A BONE TO PICK

Feasting on Shakespeare's Remains

Volume 3

written by
Sidney Wade Stout
© 2015

A Bone To Pick: Feasting on Shakespeare's Remains.
Sidney Wade Stout
Copyright © 2015

ISBN 978-0-9784483-5-6 (electronic book)
ISBN 978-0-9784483-6-3 (paperback)

All rights reserved. No part of this book may be used or reproduced by any means, graphic, electronic, or mechanical, including photocopying, recording, taping or by any information storage retrieval system without the written permission of the author except in the case of brief quotations embodied in critical articles and reviews.

Library and Archives Canada Cataloguing-in-Publication

Stout, S. W. (Sidney Wade), 1955-, author
A bone to pick: feasting on Shakespeare's remains: volume 3 / written by Sidney Wade Stout.

Includes bibliographical references.
ISBN 978-0-9784483-6-3 (paperback)

1. Shakespeare, William, 1564-1616--Criticism and interpretation. 2. Shakespeare, William, 1564-1616--Sources. 3. Shakespeare, William, 1564-1616--Stories, plots, etc. I. Title.

PR2976.S753 2015   822.3'3   C2015-905729-9

To

Janice Mackett

"some of the stupidest men are rendered more intelligent by loving"

Commentary on Plato's Symposium on Love, Speech II, Chapt. 6,
Marsilio Ficino, transl. Sears Jayne

"Thou shalt never get such a secret from me but by a parable"

W. Shakespeare
The Two Gentlemen of Verona
(2.5.34-35)

Table of Contents

A Bone to Pick: Feasting on Shakespeare's Remains — 5
    Introduction — 5

***As You Like It*: The Cure for Envy** — 6
    Introduction — 6
    Envy and Love: Obverse and Reverse — 6
    Envy at the Court — 8
    Liberty and the Arden Forest — 11
    Violence at Court — 12
    Love in the Woods — 15
    A Pattern of Protection — 16
    Rosalind and Love — 22
    A Thoughtful Distance — 24
    Conversion — 25
    Conversion and the Concept of the New World — 28
    Bruno's Innocent New World — 30
    Natural Man — 35
    Conclusion — 37
    Footnotes — 38
    Bibliography — 39

***The Two Gentlemen of Verona*: The Twin Lights of Verona** — 41
    Introduction — 41
    The Characters Come From Ficino — 42
    The Parable Comes From Aristophanes — 48
    Reprise — 52
    A Symposium on Love — 54
    Proteus and Love's Changable Nature — 57
    Rediscovering Julia — 63

Conclusion	65
Footnotes	66
Bibliography	69

***Twelfth Night*: No Darkness** — 70

Introduction	70
Delusion, Disguise and Deception	71
We Are All Asses	75
The Philosophy of the Ass	75
The Transmigration Theme	81
The Self	84
A World of Constant Change	89
What You Will	91
Conclusion	92
Footnotes	96
Bibliography	97

***The Comedy of Errors*: Cross Purposes** — 99

Introduction	99
The Dark Frame	99
Plautus' Plot	103
Biblical Allusions in a Time of Waiting	104
Inequality	115
Equity	121
Transformation	122
Enlightenment	127
Pentecost	129
Conclusion	130
Bibliography	133

***The Merry Wives of Windsor*: [Alt/Shift/Control]** — 135

Introduction	135

Enter the Cuckoo	136
Money Goes Before	138
Being Translated	139
Falstaff's Translations	142
The Skimmington	147
Rendering Justice	149
The Imaginative Landscape	150
Stories and Backstories	153
a) Mistress Quickly	153
b) Falstaff	154
c) The Host	159
d) Frank Ford	160
e) George Page	163
f) The Wives and Daughter	164
Conclusion	167
Bibliography	172

Coriolanus: The Making of Monsters — 175

Introduction	175
The Great-Souled Man	176
The Rash Man	181
The Fearful Man	187
People Hate Those Things They Fear	190
The Beast with Many Heads	196
When Monsters Meet	199
Less Than Honourable Relations	206
The Great Silence	214
Two Gods	216
Words and Actions	218
Words, Actions, Deception, and Violence	219

The Marketplace	223
Conclusion	228
Bibliography	233

A Bone to Pick: Feasting on Shakespeare's Remains

Introduction

A play is not spoiled by study. With this third volume of essays I continue to examine Shakespeare's source material with the intention of shedding some light on his possible motivation for creating the works in the first place. I want the audiences (directors and actors included) to be aware of the sub-text behind each play. It is this philosophical underpinning, that lies beneath the surface of the play, that provides the foundation upon which Shakespeare could versify. The underlying philosophy restricts and also guides the imagery so that character, plot, and symbolism might all work together in service of a central idea. It is this idea/concept that informs the plot that I am most interested in. When the effect that the author wants is made clear to the director, audience or reader it provides them with a direction to follow or an organizing principle to help make sense of the action. A director can then work out ways that draw attention or focus to the author's intent.

A play is never just entertainment, at the very least it can inform an audience, help them empathize, to rehearse a possible future where they imagine themselves in the same situation as the actors. At its best a play can become an allegory giving us direction for our lives and social policies and in effect change our world.

The following essays reveal the philosophical meat that is attached to the bones of Shakespeare's plots. It provides the nourishment that feeds our minds while we feast on his plays with our senses.

As You Like It: The Cure for Envy

Introduction

The argument put forth in this essay is that envy gives rise to the conflicts in the play and that love provides the remedy to these conflicts. Envy is the illness that infects the court while love is the atmosphere that pervades the woods. The inexplicable and rapid reversals of the characters' behaviours that make up part of the narratives become understandable when one examines the envy/love dialectic and learns to appreciate the nature of conversion.

As You Like It was written probably in 1598 along with *Julius Caesar* and prior to *Hamlet*. The play combines several traditions – folklore, classical myths, and Christian parables and blends them into a pastoral romance. *As You Like It* draws from many literary sources but it is overwhelmingly dependent on Thomas Lodge's novella *Rosalynde* (1590) for its narrative flow and on Chaucer for its structural metaphors.

Chaucer's *Canterbury Tales* provides the most probable source for the title of Shakespeare's work; for near the end of the prologue to the Wife of Bath the knight wishes to grant his wife both '*soverainte*' and '*maistry*' – '*For as you liketh, it suffiseth me*' (*As You Like It*, The Arden Shakespeare, edited by Juliet Dusinberre, Introduction, p. 2). The main story engine and the structural metaphors that permeate *As You Like It* seem to come from Chaucer's the Parson's Tale with its discussion of envy and love.

Envy and Love: Obverse and Reverse

Envy is a feeling of discontentment usually accompanied by some degree of ill-will. These feelings are elicited by the contemplation of another's good fortune or natural gifts. Unlike all the other sins envy does not even give the illusion of short-term pleasure, it only brings anguish and sorrow to its possessor.

Chaucer wrote of Envy in his *Canterbury Tales* (1387), specifically in The Parson's Tale (Sequitur de invidia)

"It is certain that envy is the worst sin that is, for all other sins are sins only against one virtue, whereas envy is against all virtue and against all goodness. For envy is bitter about all the good things that belong to another, and in this way, it is different from all other sins. For almost all other sins give some sort of pleasure in themselves, save only envy, which always has in itself anguish and sorrow".

There is an aspect of longing in envy and a sadness in the heart of the one who envies. Envy looks on those with admirable qualities – qualities which make these individuals worthy of love – and only wishes them harm. Envy evokes anger because envy destroys the tranquility of one's mind. The possessor obsesses about removing their perceived competition – this competition being for some nebulous external affirmation of love. The envious do not delight in their own abilities but rather fixate on the gifts of others and see only what is lacking in themselves. Because of this envy destroys its owner's self-esteem and steals from them their self-worth.

Envy's constant self-deprecation also invokes a consuming guilt in the envious as to why they are not better people and why they wish harm on others – particularly those who are good and essentially innocent. Because of this envy wounds self-respect and attacks the very ability to love for one cannot love others until one first loves themselves.

All is not hopeless however for as we also read in the Parson's Tale (Remedium contra peccatum inuidie) there is a remedy.

"Now will I speak of the remedy for this foul sin of envy. First, is the love of God, and the love of one's neighbour as one's self; for indeed the one cannot be without the other...Your neighbour you are bound to love

and to wish all good things; and thereunto God says, "Love thy neighbour as thyself."...Certainly, then, love is the medicine that purges the heart of man of the poison of envy."

Love honestly and sincerely wishes for the best to happen to other people and is the antithesis of envy. Just as envy destroys love so does love destroy envy. It is in this dialectic that we find the story engine for *As You Like It*. The dark aspects of the play are fueled by envy and the light aspects are fueled by love.

Envy provides the motive to both disinherit and usurp a brother as well as to banish a niece. Love provides both the cure to these problems and provides the resolution to the play.

Envy at the Court

When the play begins we are introduced to Orlando and his older brother Oliver. Oliver reveals to us that his treatment of Orlando is driven by envy (1.1.154-160)

> *for my soul*
> *– yet I know not why – hates nothing more than he. Yet*
> *he's gentle, never schooled and yet learned, full of noble*
> *device, of all sorts enchantingly beloved, and indeed so*
> *much in the heart of the world, and especially of my*
> *own people, who best know him, that I am altogether*
> *misprized* (undervalued).

Oliver hates Orlando for all the qualities that should make him love Orlando.

"*Glory and virtue (saith Virgil) are always envied: which vice is commonly accompanied with hatred and ill-will*" (*The French Academie* (1586) p. 457).

Orlando is innocent and undeserving of his brother's hatred; this is the source of his grievance with his brother. Orlando sees himself as deprived maybe even unjustly deprived. He does not hate Oliver because of this nor does he envy Oliver's advantage as first born; he merely wishes to be treated fairly so that he can go out and make his own fortune in the world (1.1.62-70)

> *My father charged you in his will to give me good*
> *education. You have trained me like a peasant,*
> *obscuring and hiding from me all gentleman-like*
> *qualities. The spirit of my father grows strong in me,*
> *and I will no longer endure it! Therefore allow me such*
> *exercises as may become a gentleman, or give me the*
> *poor lottery my father left me by testament; with that*
> *I will go buy my fortunes.*

Celia and her cousin Rosalind are foils to Oliver and Orlando. They demonstrate a healthy loving friendship that rejoices in each other's good qualities. They provide the example of mutually supportive 'sisters'. They rejoice in each other (1.2.15-16)

> *Well, I will forget the condition of my estate*
> *to rejoice in yours*

and support each other (1.2.19 20)

> *for what he hath taken away from thy father*
> *perforce, I will render thee again in affection.*

Neither Celia nor Rosalind is envious of the other. They are the healthy example of balance. Rosalind is, however, envious of something; she is envious of male advantage. This is made apparent when Rosalind discusses Fortune with Celia (1.2.34-36)

> *for her benefits are*
> *mightily misplaced and the bountiful blind woman*
> *doth most mistake in her gifts to women.*

This narrative seed will grow into Rosalind's decision to adopt a male persona when she leaves the court. It is a persona she will only drop when she learns to love herself – as she is – and is no longer envious of the male advantage.

The final example of envy at court is Duke Frederick. Early on we learn that he has usurped his older brother's natural position as ruler of the kingdom (1.1.95-96)

> *the old Duke is banished by his younger*
> *brother the new Duke.*

The new Duke, Frederick, is depicted as acquisitive and voracious driven by an envy not unlike that described in a 14th century poem by Langland, *Piers Ploughman*

> *"I could only be happy if everyone were my slave,*
> *for it drives me mad to think that anyone could*
> *have more than I have."*

Duke Frederick is driven by such an envy and tries to infect his daughter Celia with it. Envy is the reason he banishes his niece Rosalind, and he uses her good qualities to condemn her before his daughter (1.3.74-80)

> *She is too subtle for thee, and her smoothness,*
> *Her very silence and her patience*
> *Speak to the people, and they pity her.*
> *Thou art a fool. She robs thee of thy name,*
> *And thou wilt show more bright and seem more*
> *virtuous*
> *When she is gone.*

It is the Duke's perverted appreciation of people's virtues that puts Orlando in harm's way. Since Orlando is the son of the Duke's enemy (1.2.214-215) any praise he receives is perceived as praise for the Duke's enemy and hence an attack on the Duke himself, such is his madness (1.2.254-255)

> *Yet such is now the Duke's condition*

That he misconstrues all that you have done.

Orlando's success at defeating Charles, the King's wrestler, is not greeted with praise and promotion by the Duke but rather with contempt and followed by a type of banishment.

Orlando, as a character, is not motivated by envy but rather by ambition. Using Orlando as an example it is possible to highlight the distinction that exists between ambition and envy. Both want more than they have but ambition achieves its goal by bettering itself. This is what Orlando does; this is why he wants an education. He wants to rise from his untrained state of 'barnyard animal' to become a contributing member of society (1.1.6-7; 9-10)

he keeps me
rustically at home...
that differs not from the
stalling of an ox.

Envy tends to tear other people down; ambition is a process to build ourselves up. Ambition, in its purest sense, does not take away anything from somebody else; it is a self-directed internal pursuit of excellence that does not benefit from another's failure.

It is ambition that fuels Orlando into challenging the wrestler Charles. He wishes to better himself, to create an opportunity for himself, even if he has to put his own life at risk.

Liberty and the Arden Forest

The Arden woods are presented as an Eden. It is a place of freedom where social barriers dissolve, good fellowship is enjoyed and the humanities flourish. It is a place of reflection and contemplation. The first lines uttered by Duke Senior in the woods are (2.1.1)

Now, my co-mates and brothers in exile.

The old Duke has abolished rank and created a family of helpmates. Envy is fed by both hierarchy and scarcity, i.e., haves and have-nots. The old Duke in the Arden forest has removed the fuel that feeds envy. This restoration of equality marks a return to the natural state of man (*The French Academie* (1586), Chap. 43, *Of Envie, Hatred, and Backbiting*, p. 457).

"*The mind of man, which of it owne nature is created social, gracious, and ready to help everyone*".

The old Duke is described as a '*Robin Hood*' presiding over a '*golden world*' (1.1.111-113). As an audience we are assured that these woods are not a place of envy but rather are a place where liberty flourishes (1.3.134-135)

Now go we in content
To liberty and not to banishment.

To journey into the woods is to be transformed. Duke Senior is transformed into 'one of the boys', Celia becomes Aliena and is free to enjoy the company of her friend and cousin while Rosalind is allowed to entertain the fantasy of being a man. Later in the play we see two other startling transformations; they occur in the conversion experiences of Oliver (4.3.134-136) and Duke Frederick (5.4.152-163).

Violence at Court

The court appears to be under strict control by the new Duke Frederick. The flow of information seems to be reduced to hushed whispers and informal gossip. Any challengers to the new Duke are banished and their property seized (1.1.94-98)

There's no news at the court, sir, but the old
news: that is, the old Duke is banished by his younger
brother the new Duke, and three or four loving lords
have put themselves into voluntary exile with him,

whose lands and revenues enrich the new Duke.

The new Duke does not appear to be a moderate; he threatens death even upon his poor defenseless niece (1.3.39-42)

You, cousin.
Within these ten days if that thou be'st found
So near our public court as twenty miles
Thou diest for it.

In the court violence passes as entertainment. The wrestler Charles inflicts 'pain unto death' on his opponents (1.2.120-122)

Charles in a moment threw
him and broke three of his ribs, that there is little hope
of life in him.

When Oliver talks with Charles it is violence again that Charles is threatened with. Oliver contends that Orlando, if slighted, (1.1.140-143)

will practise
against thee by poison, entrap thee by some treacherous
device, and never leave thee till he hath ta'en thy life by
some indirect means or other.

Oliver is hoping to incite Charles so that he will kill Orlando in the ring (1.1.137-138)

I had as lief (I would as soon) *thou didst*
break his neck as his finger.

His envy of his brother has driven him to hate his brother and to plot his death. When 'death by wrestler' fails, Oliver then plans to kill him in his sleep (2.3.22-24)

this night he means
To burn the lodging where you use to lie,
And you within it.

Orlando is forced to flee a bad situation involving both a '*tyrant Duke*' and a '*tyrant brother*' (1.2.277) but when he flees into the woods of Arden he brings with him some of the violence of the court. His first encounter with the residents of the woods involves threatening them with violence (2.7.98-100)

> *But forbear, I say!*
> *He dies that touches any of this fruit*
> *Till I and my affairs are answered.*

He is not the only member of the court who has fled into the woods that brings a malevolent spirit with them. Touchstone, as well, threatens a gentle inhabitant, William, with violence (5.1.50-53)

> *abandon the society of*
> *this female, or, clown, thou perishest! Or to thy better*
> *understanding, diest. Or (to wit) I kill thee, make thee*
> *away, translate thy life into death.*

Even the old Duke has introduced a touch of violence into this Eden. He does so with the introduction of hunting. It is a violence against the native inhabitants of the forest, the deer. It is a violence that even the Duke is saddened by (2.1.21-24)

> *Come, shall we go and kill us venison?*
> *And yet it irks me the poor dappled fools,*
> *Being native burghers of this desert city,*
> *Should in their own confines with forked heads*
> *Have their round haunches gored.*

Jaques grieves this violence even more than the Duke (who accepts the necessity of it); Jaques feels that it is not unlike the violence Duke Frederick perpetrated on the old Duke himself (2.1.26-28)

> *The melancholy Jaques grieves at that,*
> *And in that kind swears you do more usurp*
> *Than doth your brother that hath banished you.*

Jaques sees civilization as exploiting this peaceful Eden by taking advantage of its inhabitants and adding to its own surplus (2.1.47; 48-49)

Poor deer...
giving thy sum of more
To that which had too much.

Love in the Woods

The Arden woods are presented as the destination of lovers and the habitation of gentle folk. The old Duke is accompanied into exile by '*four loving lords*' (1.1.96), Rosalind is accompanied by Celia who both loves her and gladly joins her in exile (1.1.102-104) (1.3.93-94;97) and finally the old servant Adam lovingly assists Orlando in his escape to Arden (2.3.69-70; 75-76).

The first person Touchstone, Celia, and Rosalind encounter in the woods is the lovesick Silvius (2.4.20) who reminds them of their own longings for love (2.4.41-43).

> Ros. *Alas, poor shepherd, searching of thy wound*
> *I have by hard adventure found mine own.*
> Touch. *And I mine.*

Orlando's first encounter in Arden is with the old Duke and his gentle followers who defuse his violence with their kindness (2.7.103-104)

> *Your gentleness shall force*
> *More than your force move us to gentleness.*

Orlando, once his physical needs are met, begins to mellow and nurture his romantic nature. A longing for love appears to be a side effect of entering the woods. He starts to fill the forest with poems addressed to Rosalind, his imagined and idealized love.

Many characters in the play are separated from their loved ones by some kind of distance – physical or psychological. Orlando expresses his obsession with an absent and mostly imagined love, Rosalind. Silvius tries his best to communicate his love to an unreceptive target, Phoebe, and Touchstone expresses his love to a receptive yet unappreciative audience in Audrey.

Touchstone and Orlando share the characteristic of expressing love in a way that is unappreciated. Rosalind does not appreciate Orlando's doggerel and Audrey does not appreciate Touchstone's wit.

Silvius and Orlando also share a frustration in that both express love for a person whom they feel cannot be moved to love them back, i.e., Phoebe and Ganymede/Rosalind respectively.

In addition to these obsessed lovers there are two characters that operate at some distance from love. Rosalind maintains the false persona of Ganymede in order to distance herself from Orlando's affections (while still gaining a sense of his person) and Jaques, the traveller, observes the lovers but always from a safe distance.

A Pattern of Protection

When Rosalind arms herself as a man, a hunter, (1.3.114-115; 117)

A gallant curtal-axe upon my thigh,

A boar-spear in my hand...

We'll have a swashing and a martial outside

she is not only protecting herself from possible rape (1.3.105-107) but she uses the disguise to insulate herself from love (3.2.287-288)

I will speak to him (Orlando) like a saucy lackey and

under that habit play the knave with him.

Jaques presents himself as a traveller, as such, he is a welcome outsider not expected to be involved with the life of the community. Both Jaques and Rosalind have found ways to protect themselves from what they fear. Rosalind as Ganymede is protected from male domination and love while Jaques is protected from taking any responsibility for the world around him. His cynicism isolates him and insulates him from any feelings of love for the communities he observes.

Jaques

Jaques presents himself as an outside observer. We sense that he has seen the court but has removed himself or been exiled from it, and that even though he is presently with Duke Senior and his followers he operates outside of their community as well.

Jaques' penchant for social criticism means that Jaques finds fault with even this community's gentler ways. Jaques looks on their simple happiness and finds ways to attack their innocent lives. He likens their hunting of deer to the equivalent of war waged on defenceless people (2.1.26-28; 60-64)

> *swearing that we*
> *Are mere usurpers, tyrants and what's worse,*
> *To fright the animals and to kill them up*
> *In their assigned and native dwelling-place.*

He also condemns their simple life as the choice of fools and the result of indulging their own stubborn wills (2.5.40-52).

Despite Jaques' abrasive nature he is both accepted and enjoyed for his contrary views and is often sought out by the old Duke himself (2.1.68-69)

> *I love to cope* (meet with) *him in these sullen fits,*
> *For then he's full of matter.*

Jaques pleads with the Duke for a liberty '*to speak my mind*' (2.7.59) and '*to blow on whom I please*' (2.7.47-48) but clearly he has that license already. The loving woods have provided acceptance to even such an acerbic character as Jaques.

Jaques possesses the typical characteristics that are normally assigned to melancholics (*Three Books of Occult Philosophy*, Book 1, Chpt. XXV, LII, LX, and Appendix IV); he is pensive and withdrawn. His prudence leads him to make cautious choices and this results in a pragmatic view of the world that is tainted with a realistic pessimism. In short he does not possess a lover's soul.

To give an example of how little he has in common with lovers consider his encounter with Orlando. The two are like oil and water. The joyous abandon of Orlando, '*Signior Love*' (3.2.284) is incomprehensible to Jaques and can only be viewed by him as a type of madness lacking in all logic.

Orlando cannot help but see Jaques, '*Monsieur Melancholy*', (3.2.286) as a cold fish casting a critical eye on all those around him (3.2.270-271). There is no common ground between them, they are in fact the strangest of strangers and choose to interact as little as possible (3.2.251)

> *I do desire we may be better strangers.*

Just as in *A Midsummer Night's Dream*, "*Reason and love keep little company together*" (MND 3.1.138-139).

Jaques is a social critic; he is critical but not envious of other men's fortunes. As such he questions people's innocence and calls on them to change their ways. He plays the role of the old time prophet reminding all men that they are fundamentally sinful and that they live in sin perpetually – that no one can claim innocence or be free of guilt. Jaques is a little bit 'holier than thou'; this aspect of his character is perceived by Orlando who calls him a '*painted cloth*' (3.2.266) i.e. a visual expression of a moral lesson and by the old Duke who is also quick to point out Jaques hypocrisy (2.7.64-66)

> *Most mischievous foul sin in chiding sin.*
> *For thou thyself hast been a libertine*
> *As sensual as the brutish sting itself.*

The Duke is correct in calling Jaques a libertine, for he knows Jaques has been a moral libertine in his past but he is also correct in the broader sense of the word. Jaques is a libertine in that he is responsible to no one and accountable to no authority for his actions and his comments – he is free to question any action he pleases. Because he is free of restraint and control and because he has no loyalty or roots in the community he can be seen as a 'free-thinker'. This lack of responsibility, however, breeds an irresponsible attitude in his character and this is what the old Duke takes issue with.

Jaques, in his own defense, accuses everyone of being sinful and hopes that those who see themselves reflected in his accusations will be receptive to change and adopt a new and better lifestyle. This is the point of his tirade (2.7.70-87)

If it (my condemnation) *do him right,*
Then he hath wronged himself. If he be free (of sin),
Why then my taxing (accusations) *like a wild goose flies*
Unclaimed by any man.

Conversion of others to a better life through their own recognition of their sinful nature is his goal. This is why he is so interested in Duke Frederick's conversion experience at the end of the play. He wishes to understand what brought it on (5.4.182-183)

To him will I; out of these convertites
There is much matter to be heard and learned.

Logic and reason are Jaques tools, a cynic's tools, but they will bring him very little insight into understanding the conversion experience for in this play conversion is complicit with love which lies outside the purview of logic.

Rosalind
-

Rosalind has also cooled the flame of love by placing Ganymede on guard between herself and Orlando (3.2.287-288). Rosalind, by becoming Ganymede, slows the courting process and allows a tongue-tied Orlando (1.2.246-247) the opportunity to express his feelings while at the same time gives her the chance to repress her own. Through the madness of cross-dressing Rosalind hopes to introduce some sanity in the service of love.

Previously I referred to Rosalind as suffering from a type of envy that a Freudian may refer to as 'penis envy' but it is probably better understood as an envy of male advantage. By adopting a male persona Rosalind protects herself from the threat of assault in the woods (1.3.105-107)

> *Alas, what danger will it be to us,*
> *Maids as we are, to travel forth so far!*
> *Beauty provoketh thieves sooner than gold.*

At the same time she has found a way to gain control over her relationship with Orlando, she can now watch him from the safe distance of her disguise. Using this advantage she can and does call the shots. She sets up her own engagement (4.1.114-115)

> *Come, sister, you shall be the priest and marry*
> *us. Give me your hand Orlando.*

She commands Orlando and ordains Celia. She has taken male control over society and culture. She is rehearsing a possible future; one where unheard of privileges could be wielded by women. Unfortunately in her adopted role as a man she has resorted to portraying her own sex in the most stereotyped clichés imaginable, something Celia reminds him/her of (4.1.189-190)

> *You have simply misused our sex in your love-prate!*

Rosalind plays the harsh critic of 'romantic love' in her interactions with both Orlando and Phoebe and yet she defends 'neighbourly love' in her discussion with Jaques (4.1.1-34). She attacks Jaques' melancholy or more precisely his contemplative attitude, i.e., his meditations that do not commit themselves to action. She sees Jaques as a traveller – a perpetual outsider – observing/reflecting but not participating, not physically touching, or getting physically involved in these other worlds he observes (4.1.22)

> ...*to have rich eyes and poor hands.*

When using the phrase '*poor hands*' I don't think Rosalind is referring just to wealth I think she is also using the image of the hand as a symbol for both physical and sensual involvement; hands being a common symbol signifying earthly power, strength, authority, and protection as well as symbolizing the five senses (*A Dictionary of Symbols*, Cirlot). Rosalind does not respect 'reason without action' considering it to be of no use. Jaques' travels that lead him to 'computational rumination' seem to be of no more value to Rosalind than '*a post*' (4.1.9).

Their discussion is reminiscent of 1 Corinthians 13:2

"*And though I have the gift of prophecy, and understand all mysteries, and all knowledge...and have not charity* (love)*, I am nothing*".

Love is the physical involvement with others in this world. It is not an ethereal notion of caring. This is something Jaques avoids. He remains outside of love, even neighbourly love, and constantly mocks those in love (3.2.274) considering it a personality fault.

When Rosalind tells Orlando how she will cure him of the madness of love (3.2.384) she describes how she drove one suitor (3.2.400-403)

> *from his mad humour*
> *of love to a living humour of madness, which was to*
> *forswear the full stream of the world and to live in a*
> *nook merely monastic.*

In her prescription is a possible description of Jaques' backstory – Jaques spurned by love turns melancholy and withdraws from both love and the world. In his solitude he reflects and rails at both (3.2.270-274).

In contrast Rosalind is hesitant but not afraid of love and she comes to involve herself directly in the affairs of Orlando, Silvius and Phoebe hoping to have a positive effect on their lives.

Jaques has defined himself as a spectator *"All the world's a stage..."* (2.7.140-167) and placed himself safely outside the action [1]. He watches, comments, but avoids becoming one of the actors. Even in the scene of the stag hunt (4.2) it is Jaques who directs, but does not participate in, this piece of theatre even though we know he is opposed to the hunting of deer (2.1.60-63). This is the basis of Rosalind's mild contempt for Jaques.

Rosalind and Love

Why blame you me to love you? (5.2.101)

This is the accusation Orlando makes of Rosalind, Silvius of Phoebe, and Phoebe of Ganymede. Both women hold their admirers at bay, Rosalind delays while Phoebe denies.

This accusation comes in the wake of Oliver's and Aliena's (Celia's) decision to wed. They have seen, loved, wooed, and consented to marriage unimpeded by any outside force (5.2.1-9) (5.2.28-39). Orlando sees this as the natural way that love should proceed. He sees the artificiality of his own wooing and perceives no purpose in continuing along his present course (5.2.49)

I can live no longer by thinking (imagining).

He can no longer pretend that Ganymede is Rosalind, nor can he continue to pretend that Ganymede is not Rosalind, his rehearsal period is over, and he feels now he must act. Rosalind concurs for she no longer wishes to maintain the false persona of Ganymede. She doesn't need to test Orlando further and is now willing to believe in love. At this point in the play (5.2) it is clear that both Orlando and Rosalind are suppressing a known truth, that Ganymede is Rosalind, something both know but that for different reasons neither can yet acknowledge. Shapiro (*A Year in The Life of Shakespeare: 1599*) feels that Orlando recognizes Rosalind during the mock wedding scene (4.1.119-131) and I see no cause to dispute this since it is clear that in the next scene where the two characters appear together (5.2) that they are both aware of this fact.

At Phoebe's coaxing Silvius reveals to all what it means to love (5.2.79-95) and the lovers gang up on Rosalind wanting to know what harm they do by loving. They believe that Rosalind/Ganymede and Phoebe are both blaming the victims – the victims of love – by treating them badly. They feel that love is an act of hopeful imagination in the lover and it does no harm to the object of that love.

Rosalind/Ganymede concedes and agrees to help them; she converts to their cause (5.2.106-107). Rosalind does not, as some critics suggest, alter their sense of love or cool their passions or introduce a sense of realism into their idealized longing. They are as wildly in love as they always were. Orlando would still be posting love poems all over the forest if he did not find an alternate and more effective way of wooing Rosalind and Silvius is still the lap-dog to Phoebe as Phoebe is to Ganymede.

If there is a convert in this play it is Rosalind. She begins to identify with the lovers' passions and relates to their impatience. Celia and Oliver have shown her that there is no reason for her to delay acting on her feelings of love. Love becomes the reason she drops her pretense of being a man. She is no longer envious of the privileges or protections it affords her. At this point there is nothing she wishes more than to be the woman Orlando loves and to love him fully in return. To be in love is to be vulnerable, in the thrall of another, it is a weakness all the lovers understand and accept; they are willing servants to their loves. This is why love is considered a form of justice; love is the good of others.

A Thoughtful Distance

By being Ganymede, Rosalind was not besieged by her lover as Phoebe was with Silvius. This allowed her to control the pace of her relationship with Orlando and to get a glimpse of the person behind the obsession and not just be confronted with the obsession itself. This is why Rosalind could see Orlando for the man he was and it is also how she can see Silvius for the person he is. Phoebe is not given the privilege of such a point of view for Silvius.

At this point in the play (5.2) one could say that neither Jaques nor Rosalind has had any effect on their world. Both have distanced themselves from direct involvement with it. Rosalind and Jaques are actors that put on performances for others; Jaques by wearing *'strange suits'* and adopting a *'lisp'* (4.1.30-31) plays the traveller while Rosalind plays at being a man. Both are detached characters; Jaques, as a traveller, avoids participation in the world and Rosalind, as Ganymede, avoids participation in love.

Rosalind, however, changes. Rosalind chooses to get involved – she chooses to love – by choosing to love (an internal act of conversion) she makes the world a better place for Orlando, Silvius, and presumably for Phoebe as well. She affects the world by changing herself. She is no longer envious of her male persona. She loves the woman she is and is impatient to become Rosalind again. This theme of conversion we see repeated in the play with Oliver and Duke Frederick; an individual decision, an individual act of conversion, changes the world for many others. These individual acts of internal change, authored from within and not requiring or dependent upon influencing others, initiates social change on the grand scale.

Conversion is the antithesis of Jaques' method of changing the world. He preaches change to the masses who barely acknowledge their shortcomings and who are in turn insulated by their numbers (by their society). Jaques hopes to shame them with logic and satire when in fact the best road to change may be by awakening a love within them.

Jaques and Rosalind exemplify the roles that believing and knowing play in the conversion experience. The lovers believe – they imagine – they hope for the best while Jaques attempts to know – to understand things before he commits. Rosalind converts to the lovers' side, she chooses to believe in Orlando and she asks Orlando to believe in Ganymede's magic in return. Rosalind's conversion amounts to her believing in Orlando and herself – she no longer has to be a man to accomplish her goals she believes Orlando loves the wise person she is (4.1.149).

Jaques, though intrigued by conversion is not converted during the course of the play. His character arc is uninterrupted by change. He is the same at the end of the play as at the beginning. Though he rails at the world he does not change the world. His knowledge of the world (and Jaques is wise) does not help him affect the world. The one hopeful sign for Jaques is his interest in conversion experiences; with any luck he may finally discover that the most meaningful road to social change lies within himself by choosing to love the world. If Jaques could just believe in a better world he could begin to make a better world.

Conversion

The act of conversion is not simply an act of faith but is rather an internal change of perspective. Like flicking a switch or flipping a coin, the change is immediate. All the qualities that made Orlando a subject of envy for Oliver: his nobility, his gentleness (1.1.155-160) now make him the object of Oliver's respect and love. Orlando doesn't change – it is Oliver that can now see Orlando with fresh eyes.

Orlando's kind and noble nature (4.3.127) literally saves Oliver's life (4.3.127-131) and Oliver can now see what others saw before and can love his brother for exactly those qualities. Envy has switched to Love. Oliver is proud of and rejoices in who Orlando always was.

This same conversion happens to Duke Frederick. His attack on Duke Senior's sanctuary is stopped by a re-evaluation of his own life and by reflecting on exactly the nature of the things he was about to wage war on (5.4.152-163). He realizes he was about to attack 'goodness' itself, the thing he envied in his brother he understood finally to be something to be celebrated and loved, and these qualities would make a worthy goal for his own life (5.4.179).

Rosalind's conversion is more physical and visible than these other two but no less based on a shift in perspective. Rosalind can reclaim the woman she is and wishes to be because her self-love has displaced her male envy. She is not afraid of the strong independent woman she is and she believes that Orlando loves her for it.

The magic of conversion is in its immediacy. There is no preamble, no hint of change until the change occurs. Rosalind understands the magic and mystery of this transformation. She is also aware of its near inexplicable nature. She embodies the magician to enable her own transformation (5.2.58-66). The veil of magic draws a curtain over the explanation. The transformation will occur and not be explained (5.4.137)

reason wonder may diminish.

Chaucer wrote that the cure for envy was to love thy neighbour. In Shakespeare's work the cure for much of the ills of court lie in this same admonition; to care for others is to build a just society and in justice is the whole of virtue (*Nicomachean Ethics*, Book V.i.17;19).

Throughout the play conversion has meant switching from envy to love. Oliver, Duke Frederick, and Rosalind all follow this path – the thing they envy and wish to destroy becomes the thing they embrace and love. No change occurs in the 'envied object'; the change is all in the heart of the beholder.

Oliver hates Orlando's natural inherent nobility and gentleness but comes to love his brother for these same qualities.

Duke Frederick hated and banished his older brother, Duke Senior, for the same reasons he banished Rosalind, i.e., they were both loved by the people and took the spotlight away from him. Duke Frederick, by the end of the play, comes to love his gentle and egalitarian brother and admire the caring society he created in the woods.

Rosalind, too, has passed from an envy of male privilege towards an affirmation of her own worth. She has made the journey by dressing as a man and satirizing her own sex (perhaps a manifestation of her own self-hatred, a side-effect of envy). By learning to love herself, for who she is, she has turned away from envy and towards love.

Chaucer wrote that envy was an attack on goodness itself. In the play we hear of two organized attacks. One when the old Duke usurps the forest from the deer and the other when Duke Frederick plans to usurp this same forest from his older brother. Both could be considered attacks on 'the good' – the deer as representatives of innocent nature and the old Duke and his men as representatives of an innocent people. Both are acts of envy – the destruction of the innocent – the good – in order to add to an already growing excess (2.1.47-49). Envy takes and keeps on taking and this is why love is its only cure. Love gives and keeps on giving (5.2.85). Just as envy is a turning away from the good so is love a turning towards the good.

Jaques never comes to understand the role that love plays in the conversion experience but he recognizes the power in conversion to create change. This is the difference between him and Rosalind – Rosalind understands and partakes of love while Jaques merely observes.

Conversion, however, was not just an individual experience; in 1599 it was also a consideration for foreign policy.

Conversion and the Concept of the New World

Within *As You Like It* lies the concept of a return to Eden. This is not unexpected in a pastoral romance since it harbours at its core a desire to break away from the hard realities of the present and to escape into a carefree world such as existed in a simpler time.

Arden is presented as a world quite distinct and different from the world of the court. It is presented as representative of idyllic nature with (2.1.16-17)

> *books in the running brooks,*
>
> *Sermons in stones, and good in everything.*

It is in fact the antithesis of court (2.1.3-4)

> *Are not these woods*
>
> *More free from peril than the envious court?*

Ovid writes of his current age, the Iron Age, as *'the worst of ages'*, a time when the last of the gods (Dike/Astraea/Justice) fled the earth.

> *"Now piety*
>
> *lies vanquished; and the maid Astraea, last*
>
> *of the immortals, leaves the blood soaked earth".*

Ovid saw it as an age of *'foul impiety'* full of *'fraud'*, *'deceit'*, and the *'sacrilegious love of gain'*. He saw it as the age of exploration and exploitation (*The Metamorphosis of Ovid*, translated by Allen Mandelbaum, Book 1, p.8, [Latin 127-150]).

> *"Men spread their sails before the winds,*
>
> *whose ways the mariner had scarcely learned:*
>
> *the wooden keels, which once had stood as trunks*
>
> *upon the mountain slopes, now danced upon*
>
> *the unfamiliar waves".*

Ovid's vision of the Iron Age is very much in keeping with the avaricious world that provides the back-drop to *As You Like It* and the language used in *As You Like It* is very much in keeping with the 'age of discovery' where *'men spread their sails before the winds'*.

The woods of Arden are presented as the New World and perhaps representative of the 'golden age' (1.1.112-113)

> *young gentlemen flock to him everyday and fleet the*
> *time carelessly as they did in the golden world.*

Here the native inhabitants, the deer, are seen as innocent and naïve; the citizens of their own cities which are deserted of people but peopled by deer (2.1.22-23)

> *the poor dappled fools*
> *Being native burghers of this desert city.*

Even the exiles fleeing to this Eden adopt a peaceful egalitarianism (2.1.1)

> *my co-mates and brothers in exile*

that is in keeping with their new home.

Arden is the new world to which Orlando bears the old Adam; it seems a fitting metaphor that he should be carrying the 'old Adam' to a 'new Eden' (2.7.15-17;130-134). The Arden woods are a refuge to the exiles but more than that it is seen in almost religious terms as a place of conversion and of salvation (5.4.35-36)

> *There is sure another flood toward, and these*
> *couples are coming to the ark.*

The language used by the exiles is a language peppered with images of travel and exploration. Rosalind speaks of her anticipation in the same terms as England's luck-rich dreams of discovering new lands, i.e., "*a South sea of discovery*" (3.2.192). She refers to her moods in terms of exotic animals (4.1.135-145) "*more jealous...than a Barbary cock-pigeon*", "*more clamourous than a parrot*", "*more giddy...than a monkey"*, etc. She refers to her love as unfathomable saying her (4.1.195-196)

> *affection hath an unknown*
> *bottom, like the Bay of Portugal.*

Jaques presents himself as a traveller who has both seen and contemplated upon the world (4.1.15-18). His seriousness only results in teasing from Rosalind (4.1.30-34) who shows herself to have knowledge of both traveller's affectations and the world.

England was a maritime nation and in 1599 the world was opening up daily revealing new lands to be explored and new mysteries to be investigated. It was an age of excitement and discovery; Francis Drake had circumnavigated the world in the years 1577-1580, he was the first Englishman to do so.

Drake brought back exciting news and riches from the New World; he also brought back stories of abuse of the natives by the Spanish. Debates about the religion and humanity of these new found people that lived in a virtual paradise constituted a part of daily discussion by 1599 (*The Secret Voyage of Sir Francis Drake: 1577-1580*, Samuel Bawlf, Walker Publishing Co. Inc., 2003).

I believe that Shakespeare's empathetic and moving discussion delivered by Jaques about the 'deer of Arden' (2.1.21-24; 26-43; 60-63) can really be understood as applying to the native people of the Americas. Such empathy for deer in the hunting culture of 1599 would certainly have been a minority opinion but when seen as an allegory for the exploitation and displacement of natives of other lands it takes on more gravity and relevance.

Bruno's Innocent New World

When Rosalind adopts the name Ganymede (son of Tros, of the house of Troy) for her male persona she is alluding to Jove's cupbearer

(*Iliad*, 20.268-272, R. Fagels) and by choosing it Shakespeare was certainly adding a dimension of homoerotic tension to the script. He was also doing one other thing; he was alluding to the constellation Aquarius which was understood to represent Ganymede.

"Aquarius (The Constellations 26)

...the figure represented is Ganymede, and they call Homer to witness..."

from *The Constellations* of Pseudo-Eratosthenes (first/second century C.E.)

"Aquarius

Many say this is Ganymede...

Hegesianax, however, says the figure is Deucalion because, during his reign, such a quantity of water fell from heaven that a great flood reportedly occurred".

from *Poetic Astronomy* 2.29 by Hyginus (first century B.C.E.).

In G. Bruno's poem *The Expulsion of the Triumphant Beast* (*Lo Spaccio de la bestia trionfante*) (1584) (Third Dialogue: second part, A.D. Imerti, p. 249-250) Bruno gives Aquarius the job of visiting the men of earth to reveal certain truths to them.

"And let it no longer be believed (that the great flood) to have been a particular deluge, since it is thought impossible that the sea and the rivers could have covered both hemispheres, or even one on this side of, and beyond, the Tropics or the Equinox...

"He should give them to understand that a new part of the earth, called the New World, has been recently discovered, that there they have memorials of ten thousand years and more..."

Bruno's reference to certain ten thousand year old memorials is to the discovery by the Spanish of the circular Aztec Calendar Stone found in Tenochtitlán in 1521, a calendar that ecclesiastical authorities decided to reinter in 1558 to avoid the very questions about the flood that Bruno raised in his poem (see note 52, p.307 of Imerti's translation, fortunately for history the stone was rediscovered in 1790).

Shakespeare in *As You Like It* has subtly engaged Bruno. Shakespeare has referred to Noah's ark (5.3.35-36), mentioned the age of the earth (4.1.86-87)

> *The poor world is*
> *almost six thousand years old*

and has done this so as to broaden the discussion around the question of native innocence (2.1.22-63). It forces one to ask whether the flood was universal or whether it just happened in one part of the world. It also implies that the natives of the Americas were not sinful because their part of the world was not destroyed by God in the Great Flood. If Bruno's argument is true then how should this affect our treatment of them?

Bruno published six books while in England (1583-1585). They were published by John Charlewood under the fictitious foreign imprint of being printed in Venice (possibly to avoid the taint of Protestantism that an English imprint would carry). These works are:

La Cena de le ceneri (The Ash Wednesday Supper)

De la causa, principio et uno (Cause, Principle and Unity)

De l'infinito, universo et mundi (On the Infinite Universe and Worlds)

Lo Spaccio de la bestia trionfante (The Expulsion of the Triumphant Beast)

la Cabala del cavallo pegaseo con l'aggiunta dell'Asino cillenico (The Cabala of Pegasus with The Cyllenic Ass)

Gli Eroici furori (The Heroic Furors or The Heroic Enthusiasts)

The published Bruno was certainly known by Shakespeare and his ideas found a home in several of his plays. When Shakespeare wrote *Love's Labour's Lost* I argued that he incorporated Bruno's philosophy of universal matter into the play (*In Sheep's Clothing*, essay entitled

'Bruno's Labour's Not Lost', p.190-214,). With *As You Like It* I intuit that he is again insinuating one of Bruno's philosophies, this time one about the age of the earth and the extent of the flood, into his work.

In both plays there is an undercurrent that is at odds with religious orthodoxy. *Love's Labour's Lost* argues that matter carries with it no taint of sin and that the same matter makes up God, the stars, the planets, the earth, and ourselves. In *As You Like It* I believe the age of the world and the extent of Noah's flood are being contested, and the innocence of the indigenous people is proposed. This is not done overtly but is hinted at with subtle reference to Bruno's poems; the age of the world (4.1.86-87), Noah's flood (5.4.35-36) and the deer as native inhabitants (2.1.22-63) all are alluded to in the play, a play that foregrounds both travel and the New World.

Bruno's poem *Lo Spaccio* (*The Expulsion of the Triumphant Beast*) is an homage to the natural religion of the Egyptians, a religion that sees god in all nature; not unlike Duke Senior (2.1.16-17)

> *books in the running brooks,*
> *Sermons in stones, and good in everything.*

One last feature shared by Bruno and Shakespeare is an apparent preoccupation with deer and the Actaeon legend. *Love's Labour's Lost* and *As You Like It* both allude to this myth as does Bruno's *Gli Eroici furori* (*The Heroic Furors* or *The Heroic Enthusiasts*). In Shakespeare's dramas the deer play an important role; both his romances make puns using 'deer' and 'dear' as well as with 'hart' and 'heart', e.g., (3.2.238-239) but both have serious allusions to Actaeon as well.

The Actaeon legend (*The Metamorphosis of Ovid*, translated by Allen Mandelbaum, p.81-86, Latin [125-260]) tells the story of a hunter who while hunting deer comes across the naked Diana bathing. For the crime of spying on her Diana turns Actaeon into a deer which is then chased and eaten by his own dogs. Bruno interprets this legend in a very particular way (*The Heroic Enthusiasts*, The first part, fourth dialogue, L. Williams translation, p. 91-94). Bruno believes the parable is about finding god within ourselves, i.e., within our own natures (*In Sheep's Clothing*, Stout, p.140-141; p.203-205). Actaeon when out hunting (looking for nature) sees Diana, the goddess of nature, naked, i.e., her secrets revealed. While seeking nature he has stumbled across the secret knowledge of nature or stated differently he has discovered the divine ideas behind natural creation. He sees that nature is linked to the divine. Actaeon has an epiphany, one he cannot unlearn. This is in fact a conversion experience. He has seen behind the curtain. He has learned that he is a part of both nature and the divine. So Actaeon learns that he is nature (the deer) and that he is also god in that he is privy to the secrets linking nature to divinity; so to understand god all he needs to do is to look within himself. His thoughts (his dogs) turn inward to discover the god within. He is consumed by these thoughts and is now dead to the material world because he now lives to understand the divine, which can be found within himself.

Allusion to Ovid's legend can be found in the several 'Actaeon-like' transformations that occur in *As You Like It*: first, the deer are regarded by Jaques as people (2.1.45-63) and then Jaques is seen as being one of them (2.7.1-2)

> *I think he* (Jaques) *be transformed into a beast*
> *For I can nowhere find him like a man.*

Later in the play they dress up a hunter like a deer (4.2.10-11)

> *What shall he have that killed the deer?*
> *His leather skin and horns to wear.*

But this is not the last of the allusions for Rosalind is part of a visual convergence that links a tearful Diana (4.1.143-144)

> *I will weep for nothing,*
> *like Diana in the fountain*

with a tearful deer (2.1.38-39;40;42-43)

> *...the big round tears*
> *coursed one another down his innocent nose*
> *In piteous chase. And thus the hairy fool...*
> *Stood on th'extremest verge of the swift brook,*
> *Augmenting it with tears.*

When Bruno interpreted the Actaeon legend he saw it as a tale about the epiphany of self-enlightenment. *As You Like It* shares this thematic connection with Bruno's poem. Much of the action in *As You Like It* revolves around the idea of conversion, an action that is presented as mysterious, magical and that occurs in an instant. Just as in Bruno's poem it is seen as an internal experience that changes a person into a completely new person, an action that is followed by a turning towards the divine. It is seen as an act of love. In *As You Like It* conversions happen to Oliver, Duke Frederick and to Rosalind.

Natural Man

As You Like It never explicitly argues that 'natural man' is generous and kind but Shakespeare does employ the old Duke and his men as examples of such an idea and Shakespeare also shows Orlando believing in the falsity that natives are savage (2.7.108)

> *I thought that all things had been savage here.*

Civilization is in turn presented as the great corruptor, *'the envious court'* (2.1.4), and the breeder of hatreds. One scene that brings this out is played between Touchstone and Corin (3.2.11-82).

Corin is a native of Arden, he is a *'natural philosopher'* and he deals in simple truths. One gets the impression he has observed nature and learned from it and from others in his community but that he is formally unschooled. Despite lack of training (like Orlando) we see that he knows God and loves his neighbours (3.2.70-72)

I earn that I eat, get that
I wear; owe no man hate, envy no man's happiness;
glad of other men's good.

Touchstone tells this good man that he is damned because he is uncivilized, i.e., he (3.2.38-42)

never sawst good manners

and therefore his

manners must be wicked, and
wickedness is sin and sin is damnation.

This of course was the one of the positions argued about the natives of the Americas. One group argued that they were innocent and therefore knew no sin – like children – and that they lived in a world that was not punished by the flood and grew up knowing God through nature. They were responsible to God only for the revelation they received.

The other group argued that they were pagans, uncivilized, sinful, and would be condemned to hell if not given the instruction of the Church to help with their salvation – the 'missionary position' as it were.

A similar position to these is expressed in the dairies of Francis Fletcher, the Cambridge-educated chaplain that accompanied Drake on his circumnavigation of the world (*The Secret Voyage of Sir Francis Drake: 1577-1580*, Bawlf, p.83)

"Fletcher found the natives' manners and religion repugnant writing that they performed the necessities of nature and even copulated in full view of bystanders, and offered the most loathsome sacrifices to their god, the sun. Still, he wrote, he preferred these primitive creatures of nature who worshipped the sun out of simple ignorance to the supposedly civilized papists, who professed to have the keys to all knowledge and power of heaven and hell, and yet venerated wooden idols".

Shakespeare's natives are like Corin; they are innocent as the deer. Their actions appear to arise out of kindness. They have no formal training and are in need of no instruction. They are presented as a group that is being increasingly threatened and exploited by the encroaching civilization.

Conclusion

The play, like all Shakespeare's plays, does not directly address any particular issues but gently alludes to them as it does to the related works of other authors. The controversies that arise out of the discovery of the New World and the questioning of ecclesiastical authority, all form a backdrop to a play that is essentially about the conversion experience. An experience which can turn envy into love and transform the convertites into new people. The play speaks more generally of love as a force that turns us towards the good. This concept that 'love was the first turning towards the good' can be found in Ficino's *Commentary on Plato's Symposium on Love* (I.3). That love is central to a pastoral romance is no great revelation but that it plays a central role to the conversion experience is a more powerful message.

Love as the first turning towards the good means that love is a far more effective tool than reason or force is in trying to convert a people or to create a social change. This controversial lesson could be applied equally to both secular and religious governance in a time of both religious dissention and explorational conquest (2.7.103-104)

> *Your gentleness shall force*
> *More than your force move us to gentleness.*

Footnotes

[1] In Francis Yate's book *Theatre of the World* (p.165-167) she points out a possible source for Jaques speech on *"All the world's a stage..."* (2.7.140-167). She draws our attention to a book *Theatre of Human Life* or *Theatrum vital humanae* printed in 1596. It was an emblem book that consisted of a series of engraved pictures accompanied by poems and prose discourses in Latin. Boissard wrote the poems and prose while Theodore De Bry made the engravings.

The first emblem in the book is called the 'Theatre of Human Life', the first line of the accompanying poem states *"The life of man is like a circus, or a great theatre"* and the image shows a vast audience watching from the galleries of a theatre the miseries in the life of a man, i.e., his temptation, sin and death. In the prose commentary that follows Boissard goes through the seven ages of man, from cradle to grave.

The speech by Jaques in *As You Like It* follows this formula very closely.

Bibliography

1) *As You Like It*, W. Shakespeare, edited by Juliet Dusinberre, The Arden Shakespeare, 3rd Series, Thompson Learning, 2007.
2) *The Nicomachean Ethics*, Aristotle, translation by H. Rackham, The Loeb Classical Library, Harvard University Press, 1956.
3) *The Seven Deadly Sins*, Ideas, The Canadian Broadcasting Corporation, Jan. 2,9,16,23,30, Feb. 6,13, 1989, CBC transcripts.
4) *The French Academie* (1586), Peter de la Primaudaye, Georg Olms Verlag Press, 1972.
5) *Canterbury Tales*, Geoffrey Chaucer, The Parson's Tale, Modern Language Edition, http://classiclit.about.com.
6) *A Dictionary of Symbols*, J.E. Cirlot, translated by Jack Sage, Philosophical Library, Routledge and Kegan Paul Ltd., 1962.
7) *A Year in the Life of William Shakespeare: 1599*, James Shapiro, HarperCollins Publishers, 2006.
8) *Three Books of Occult Philosophy*, Henry Cornelius Agrippa, translated by James Freake, edited and annotated by Donald Tyson, Llewellyn Publications, 2004.
9) *Star Myths of the Greeks and Romans*: A Source book containing *The Constellations* of Pseudo-Eratsothenes and the *Poetic Astronomy* of Hyginus, translation and commentary by Theony Condos, Phanes Press, 1997.
10) *The Expulsion of the Triumphant Beast* (*Lo Spaccio de la bestia trionfante*), Giordano Bruno, transl. by Arthur D. Imerti, University of Nebraska Press, 2004.
11) *The Heroic Enthusiasts an Ethical Poem* (*Gli Eroici furori*), Giordano Bruno, translation by L Williams, (facsimile copy of an 1887 publication), Kessinger Publishing, 2005.

12) *Commentary on Plato's Symposium on Love*, Marsilio Ficino, translated by Sears Jayne, Spring Publications, Inc., 1985.
13) *In Sheep's Clothing: The Arcane, Profane and Subversive in Shakespeare*, S. Stout, Greenbeast design inc., 2008.
14) *The Metamorphosis of Ovid*, translated by Allen Mandelbaum, A Harvest Book, Harcourt Inc., 1993.
15) *The Secret Voyage of Sir Francis Drake: 1577-1580*, Samuel Bawlf, Walker Publishing Co. Inc., 2003.
16) *The Iliad*, Homer, translated by Robert Fagles, Penguin Books, 1998.
17) *Theatre of the World*, F.A. Yates, Routledge & Kegan Paul Inc. in association with Methuen Inc., 1987.

The Two Gentlemen of Verona: **The Twin Lights of Verona**

Introduction

The Two Gentlemen of Verona is often classified as belonging to a group of stories that examine the dialectic between love and friendship. Although ideas relating to the friendship tradition can be seen in Shakespeare's source material, the story of Titus and Gisippus (Book 2, Chapter 12) as told in Sir Thomas Elyot's *The Boke Named the Governour* (1531), I do not believe the same can be said about *The Two Gentlemen of Verona* itself. Rather *Two Gentlemen* is better understood as one of the plays heavily influenced by Ficino's *Commentary on Plato's Symposium on Love* (*De Amore*). It is the theme of betrayal and redemption as told by Aristophanes (Speech IV) and translated by Ficino that dominates Shakespeare's story engine and gives rise to the action in the play.

De Amore was widely known in France and England during the 16th and 17th centuries and was an influence on many of the poets of Shakespeare's day; Spenser, Sidney, and Chapman all bear his mark (*Commentary on Plato's Symposium on Love*, Marsilio Ficino, translated by Sears Jayne, Introduction, V. Subsequent History, p. 19-23). The fact that Ficino's ideas were so widely dispersed meant that writers often used these ideas without being aware of their source. Despite this fact I believe in Shakespeare's case I can show that it was *De Amore* that informed the construction of both his characters and their relationships in the play. As you follow both Shakespeare's dramatization and Ficino's commentary on Plato it will become apparent that Shakespeare echoes Ficino in many key areas and that our knowledge of Ficino enhances our understanding and appreciation of Shakespeare's tale.

The healing nature of Love is revealed by Shakespeare and Ficino and in both works the tale is told as an allegory hidden just below its rough surface (2.5.34-35)

Thou shalt never get such a secret from me but by
a parable.

Both Shakespeare and Ficino followed this same practice (Ficino, Speech IV, Chpt. 1, p. 72)

"it was the custom of the ancient theologians to conceal their holy and pure mysteries in the shadows of metaphors".

The Characters Come From Ficino

Ficino relates to us a story told by Aristophanes (Speech IV, Chpt. 1, p.71-73) in his commentary. It is about the two lights that are held within each human being – one the light of reason (the innate, human, natural light) and the other the light of intuition (the divine, infused light). Aristophanes relates the story thusly:

"In the beginning there were three genders of human beings, not only two as now, male and female, but there existed a certain third, composed of both".

These beings were *"provided with two lights, one innate and the other infused, in order that by the innate light they may perceive inferior and equal things, and by the infused, superior things".*

But these beings, he argued, *"They turned themselves towards the innate light alone"* and *"lost the infused splendor when they were turned towards the innate light alone, and they fell immediately into bodies"* and by this he means the souls, already divided, began to focus only on the sensual world.

Aristophanes goes on to tell us

"They had three sexes: male born of the sun; female, of the earth; and mixed, of the moon. Some received the splendor of God as courage,

which is male; others as Temperance, which is female; others as Justice, which is mixed".

Aristophanes elaborates (Speech IV, Chpt. 5, p. 77)

"...we are led by four virtues: Prudence, Courage, Justice, and Temperance. Prudence...shows us bliss; those other three virtues, like three paths, lead to bliss. And so God tempers his own spark variously in various souls to this end, that under the direction of Prudence some seek their author again through the offices of Courage, others through the offices of Justice, and others through the offices of Temperance". [1]

And so *"some, thanks to this gift, undergo dangers and death with a brave heart...Others arrange life so justly that they neither themselves do harm to anyone nor, insofar as possible, permit it to be done by others. Others master the appetites by vigil, fast, and work. These certainly proceed by three paths, but they all strive to arrive at the same end of bliss".*

Aristophanes repeats

"The Courage of men we call masculine because of its hardness and boldness. Temperance we call feminine because of a certained restrained and cooler habit of desire and its soft nature. Justice we call mixed. Feminine...because of its innocence it brings harm to no one. But masculine inasmuch as it does not permit harm to be done to others".

It is from these defining characteristics that the play's major characters spring. Valentine is defined by Courage, Silvia by Temperance, and Julia by the mixed quality of Justice.

Valentine's courage drives him to seek adventure and advancement (1.1.63; 64)

He after honour hunts...
He leaves his friends to dignify them more.

He wishes to find a place for himself in the outside world, away from family and friends. His leave taking is a courageous act; it puts him in the company of other adventurous men (1.3.8-10)

> *Some to the wars to try their fortune there;*
> *Some to discover islands far away;*
> *Some to the studious universities.*

Valentine is not content to stay at home, he wants (1.1.6)

> *To see the wonders of the world abroad.*

Valentine's courageous nature is seen throughout the play. It is apparent in his plans to elope with Silvia by climbing to her window (2.4.177-180) as well as in his behaviour when he is seized upon by the Outlaws (4.1). He is also lion-hearted in his defense of Silvia against Proteus (5.4.60-70) and in finally driving Turio away (5.4.124-125)

> *Turio, give back, or else embrace thy death;*
> *Come not within the measure of my wrath.*

Valentine's boldness does not waiver even when dealing with Silvia's father, the Duke, as he procures pardons for both himself and the other outlaws (54.150-156). Valentine embodies the male virtue of Courage.

Silvia is the feminine virtue of Temperance. Her soft habits and cooler desire give shape to her restrained character. We sense her coolness and her sense of humour when she gets Valentine to write a love letter essentially to himself (2.1.155)

> *Herself hath taught her love himself to write unto her*
> *lover.*

Silvia is gracious (2.4.104)

> *Too low a mistress for so high a servant*

when first meeting Proteus. She flatters him by acknowledging all the praises Valentine has used in describing him. Later she reveals herself to be self aware and therefore not easily moved by Proteus' compliments for she is not (4.2.93-94)

> *so shallow, so conceitless,*
> *To be seduced by thy flattery.*

She dismisses his advances and yet tempers her judgment against him by granting his request for a picture of herself (4.2.125-128)

> *I am very loath to be your idol, sir.*
> *But, since your falsehood shall become you well*
> *To worship shadows and adore false shapes,*
> *Send to me in the morning, and I'll send it.*

Silvia, when she decides to run away in search of Valentine, does so in a temperate manner. She will go with protection and be accompanied by a knight (4.3.22-26)

> *Sir Eglamour, I would to Valentine*
> *To Mantua, where I hear he makes abode;*
> *And for the ways are dangerous to pass*
> *I do desire thy worthy company,*
> *Upon whose faith and honour I repose.*

This is unlike Julia's behaviour when, under similar circumstances, she chose to strike off on her own dressed as a man.

Silvia also reveals her temperate spirit when abducted by the Outlaws for she patiently endures the trial (5.3.15)

> *O Valentine, this I endure for thee!*

Her love for Valentine fills her but does not make her reckless (5.4.36-38)

> *O heaven, be judge how I love Valentine,*
> *Whose life's as tender to me as my soul!*
> *And full as much, for more there cannot be.*

Julia derives her character from Justice which was considered a virtue that mixed the feminine (that innocence which wishes to harm no one) with the masculine (that which does not permit harm to be done to others). These attributes are certainly embodied in the Julia/Sebastian personae.

At the beginning of the play Julia initiates the judging of potential lovers by asking Lucetta her opinion of the various suitors (1.2.4;6)

Of all the fair resort of gentlemen
In thy opinion which is the worthiest love?

From Lucetta's reply Julia fears she is being manipulated for – coincidence upon coincidence – Lucetta just happens to deliver a letter from the gentleman she has just praised as most worthy. Because of this perceived bias Julia tears up the letter before reading it. However feeling she acted unjustly and impulsively she attempts to restore it (1.2.119)

Till I have found each letter in the letter.

In this act Julia has revealed her innocence and her unwillingness to harm anyone and perhaps anything as she tries to reassemble the letter to its previous condition, not wishing to damage even the recorded thoughts of another.

Julia as Sebastian then acts to prevent harm being done to others. S/he courts for Proteus; as his servant justice demands that she do as he bids (4.4.88)

How many women would do such a message?

but as his lover she hopes to do it poorly (4.4.104)

Yet will I woo for him, but yet so coldly.

Julia acts with an innocence so as to cause harm to no one and no thing. Even when presented with a picture of Silvia to deliver to Proteus she acts against her own desires and takes care of the object (4.4.200-202)

I'll use thee kindly for thy mistress' sake
That used me so; or else, by Jove I vow,
I should have scratched out your unseeing eyes.

In the final act Justice really comes down to how Julia will react to Proteus' repeated acts of betrayal. Julia has not only heard reports of Proteus' unfaithfulness but she has witnessed it first-hand. She is called on by Valentine and her conscience to behave in a manner characteristic of a merciful god (5.4.79-80)

Who by repentance is not satisfied
Is nor of heaven nor earth, for these are pleased.

She is the aggrieved party that must grant forgiveness by Grace to Proteus. Proteus has repented but not done any penance for his sins. Grace is the only thing that can restore him and it is up to Julia once again to pick up the pieces. In this last scene Julia embodies both Justice and Grace and to emphasize the point repeated puns are made along this line (5.4.163-164)

Duke: *I think the boy hath grace in him...*
Val.: *I warrant you, my lord, more grace than boy.*

This leaves us with Proteus. He is the prototype for all humankind. He is the changeable creature God created capable of exercising its own free will in any way it should choose. In this play he has three friends that can help guide him to bliss; Valentine (Courage), Silvia (Temperance) and Julia (Justice). I believe that Proteus' tale has more to do with the parable of the prodigal son (forgiveness by Grace) than it has to do with the tales of friendship that Shakespeare utilized for its outline (*The Two Gentlemen of Verona*, The Arden Edition, edited by William C. Carroll, Introduction, The Early Modern Discourse of Male Friendship, p. 3-23). Even Carroll points out in his introduction (p. 31) that the bond between Proteus and Valentine is not of the type idealized in the friendship tradition. The forgiveness and acceptance Proteus receives at the end of the play has more to do with love than with familiarity. A distinction made clear in Ficino's Commentary (Speech IV, Chpt. 6, p. 79)

"...we do not embrace with love those who have known us, but only those who have loved us. For many of those who know us we regard as enemies. Therefore what restores us to heaven is not knowledge of God but love".

Proteus is loved by Julia and Valentine; both have full knowledge of his betrayals; both have been eyewitness to the events; both have every reason to regard him as an enemy but both possess the love to restore him (Speech IV, Chpt. 1, p.71)

"Love is especially generous to mankind; a guardian, protector, and physician to men".

This is why I believe that the central parable is that of a return to grace – to bliss – and not one arising from the friendship tradition. Love not knowledge, familiarity, or kinship is the key to Proteus' reinstatement.

The Parable Comes From Aristophanes

Proteus is not only the prototype human he is also symbolic of the 'fallen man'. Aristophanes previously told us of how each of us was born with two lights; how our 'free will' led us to ignore one of these lights and by so doing led to our fallen state (Speech IV, Chpt. 4-5, p.76)

"But it has been decreed by Providence that the soul should be mistress of itself, and be able to use sometimes both lights at once and sometimes one...

But our soul fell into the body when, neglecting the divine light, it used its own light alone and began to be <u>content with itself</u>. Only God, to whom nothing is lacking...remains content with Himself, sufficient to Himself. Therefore <u>the soul made itself equal to God</u> when it wished to be content with itself alone...

Aristophanes says that this pride was clearly the cause of the soul...being split, that is, with regard to its twin lights; after this it used one but neglected the other"

or stated another way

"As soon as we turned to the natural light, we neglected that infused and divine light. Therefore the one having been disdained, we kept the other. Where we keep one-half of ourselves, we have lost the other half..."

Proteus is the earthly bound man who has isolated himself (2.6.19)

Julia I lose, and Valentine I lose.

This picture is reinforced later in the play when he declares both Julia and Valentine to be dead (4.2.103; 109)

But she is dead.

I likewise hear that Valentine is dead.

Proteus is <u>content with himself</u> (2.6.23)

I to myself am dearer than a friend.

His own self-interest has become his only motivation and that interest is focused on the sensual world. This is why Proteus symbolizes the fallen man but not only the fallen man, Proteus also is symbolic of the changeable, corrupt, sensual body, the material mass separated from its own soul. Let Aristophanes explain (Speech IV, Chpt. 3, p.75)

"Therefore Man is the soul alone; the body is merely a work and instrument of Man...therefore the soul can take the name of Man as proper to itself, independent of the mass of the body.

Since each of us throughout our entire life is called "Man", at any age, then surely this name seems to signify something that remains fixed. <u>*The body is perpetually in flux*</u>*, changed by growing and shrinking...The soul always remains the same...*

Who, therefore, will be so foolish as to attribute the appellation of Man, which is firmly fixed in us, to <u>the body, which is always flowing and everywhere changed</u>, rather than to the most stable soul?"

The body is not only fickle and changable it is also blamed for the soul's forgetfulness, for when the soul (Speech IV, Chpt. 5, p.76)

"Plunged into the abyss of the body as though into the river Lethe, and forgetting itself for a time, it is seized by the senses and lust".

Proteus suffers this same amnesia when confronted with the beauty of Silvia (2.4.189-191)

As one nail by strength drives out another,
So the remembrance of my former love
Is by a newer object quite forgotten.

He is seized by the body, the senses and his lust for Silvia and forgets the constancy he swore to Julia (2.2.8).

Aristophanes' story teaches us that twin lights dwell in each of us as individuals and that we can restore our right standing with God by turning toward the divine light within our own selves and balancing this with the innate light. Proteus increasingly turns away from the divine light, symbolized by his turning away from Julia, and turns towards the innate light of the world. The innate light makes him selfish and forgetful as he begins to reflect only on his needs. In this act of pride he isolates himself, makes himself his own god, and begins his downward spiral.

Proteus' redemption starts when his immoral behaviours are witnessed by both Valentine and Julia. He is shamed and forced to acknowledge his own actions – shocked into self-awareness. It is at this point that he is capable of change. Aristophanes observed (Speech IV, Chpt. 5, p.77)

> *"...when the body has matured, and the instruments of the senses have been purged...the soul's intellect is very strongly goaded, by the prodding of its own light, to recover the divine light".*

Proteus, begins to remember Julia, by first touching her ring and then by touching her; he begins to engage his higher senses and finally his reason. He can now empathize with another, with one he loved and betrayed, and all the more shamefully because he learns he betrayed her in her presence. Caring for another helps put his life back into a proper balance where he can once again use both his innate natural light and the infused light to recover his integrity. The constancy Proteus sees as his salvation is not one of behaviour but of goal orientation. If one pegs their behaviour in the service of the divine (the constant goal) then one can adapt to a changing world without ever falling into sin. We know in Justice is the sum of all virtue and that justice is the good of others – it is a giving up of selfishness (*Nicomachean Ethics*, Book V.i.17;19). Proteus' redemption reveals the secret to a life free of corruption (5.4.109-111)

> *...were man*
> *But constant, he were perfect. That one error*
> *Fills him with faults.*

Valentine's and Silvia's relationship is the model of balance and selflessness. Valentine essentially vanishes (3.1.170-172; 182-184; 214) when Silvia is taken from him. Both care for the other as themselves (5.4.36-37)

> *O heaven, be judge of how I love Valentine,*
> *Whose life's as tender to me as my soul!*

Each is the divine light for the other that balances their own innate light and prevents the insular selfishness that Proteus falls into.

Reprise

Lance's journey parallels and echoes, in a comic way, the journey made by the other characters in the play. He provides some of the emotional context that is lacking with the other more stoic characters in the play.

The departure of a son, a daughter, or a brother is clearly distressing for a family and a cause of great sadness. While these emotions are temperately expressed at Valentine's, Proteus', or Julia's departures they are given full expression at Lance's leaving home. Lance, too, is distressed at having to leave his loving home (2.3.49-51)

> *if the river were*
> *dry, I am able to fill it with my tears; if the wind were*
> *down, I could drive the boat with my sighs.*

The only living creature not distressed at his leaving is Crab, his dog, *"the sourest-natured dog that lives"* (2.3.5). In the scenes with Lance and Crab, Lance essentially takes on the role of Julia and Crab, the dog, plays Proteus. The dog represents the selfish beast Proteus has become. He does not *"shed one tear"* at Lance's leaving nor does Proteus when he leaves Julia. Yet Julia, like Lance, sheds a *"tide of tears"* (2.2.14) at Proteus' parting.

Lance is as forbearing with Crab's bad behaviour at court as Julia is of Proteus'. Lance loves Crab and protects him from harm (4.4.13-15)

> *If I had not had more wit than he, to take a fault*
> *upon me that he did, I think verily he had been hanged*
> *for't; sure as I live, he had suffered for't*

and again (4.4.28-30)

> *How many masters would do this for his*
> *servant? Nay, I'll be sworn I have sat in the stocks for*
> *puddings he* (Crab) *hath stolen.*

Compare this with Julia's complaint (4.4.88)

How many women would do such a message?

as she delivers a love letter and ring from her love, Proteus, to his new love, Silvia. Just like Lance loves Crab so Julia loves Proteus (4.4.94)

Because I love him, I must pity him.

This ability of love to look past the faults of others is found throughout the play. Speed refers to love as the 'deforming eye' and tells Valentine that he cannot see Silvia for what she is because love has deformed her in his eyes for *"if you love her you cannot see her"* (2.1.64).

This is also apparent with Lance and the 'cate-log' (list of qualities) he has produced of the woman he is in love with. As he goes through the list of her virtues and vices with Speed he slowly changes all her vices into virtues and instead of objectively assessing her he convinces himself he loves her even more (3.1.269-355).

Julia, as the play proceeds, also witnesses Proteus' increasing betrayals of herself and his friend. She is not naïve about what Proteus has done but still she loves him as Lance does his dog and his mistress – unconditionally.

This is a manifestation of the quality of justice (the good of others) that Julia is modelled on. Ficino elaborates on this very quality of Love (Ficino, Speech V, Chpt. 8, p.96)

"Love is affirmed as just for this reason, that where love is pure and true, there is an interchange of good will which admits no insult or injury. So great is the power of this charity that it alone is able to preserve the human in tranquil peace, which neither prudence nor fortitude, nor the power of arms...can bring about".

This helps explain why Julia's love is not deterred by Proteus' actions.

Reference to Ficino also explains why Silvia instinctively takes an early dislike to Proteus. It is a result of Silvia's temperate nature

"Moreover, he calls it temperate because it conquers the base desires. For since love seeks beauty, which consists in a certain order and temperance, it scorns cheap and intemperate appetites; it always shrinks from sinful actions".

A Symposium on Love

The Greek word *'heros'* means *'love'* (Speech VI, Chpt. 5, p.113) and love is the hero in Shakespeare's play and hence his dependence on *Ficino's Commentary on Plato's Symposium on Love* [2]. As Ficino's commentary moves from specific speeches on specific topics to more general characteristics common to the love experience he teaches us what love is capable of. It is Ficino's examination of these subjects that helps us to elucidate *The Two Gentlemen of Verona* and that also hints at Shakespeare's familiarity with Ficino's text.

Ficino understands love (Speech VI, Chpt. 5, p.113) as *"midway between formlessness and form"* an idea that matches Proteus' shape-shifting journey. At the beginning of the play Valentine challenges Proteus to come join him (1.1.5-8)

I rather would entreat thy company
To see the wonders of the world abroad
Than, living dully sluggardized at home,
Wear out thy youth with shapeless idleness.

Proteus begins our play as shapeless, formless, even his father perceives this and realizes that only action can shape his boy into something of value (1.3.20-22)

...he cannot be a perfect man
Not being tried and tutored in the world.
Experience is by industry achieved.

Proteus has the majority of lines in the play, he is the main character and his journey is the focus of Shakespeare's work. He is the 'bad lover' who will learn what true love is. Like all lovers he shares in the same obsessive characteristics as they do (Speech VI, Chpt. 10, p.125)

"The same love which makes a lover careless and indolent in other affairs makes him clever and crafty in affairs of love, so that in marvelous ways he goes bird-catching for the beloved's favor, whether he snares him with traps, or captures him with attentions, or appeases him with eloquence, or soothes him with song".

The text of '*Two Gentlemen*' bears witness to this assignment for Proteus has become a lover careless and indolent in his own life (1.1.65-69)

> *I leave myself, my friends and all, for love*
> *Thou, Julia, thou hast metamorphosed me:*
> *Made me neglect my studies, lose my time,*
> *War with good counsel, set the world at naught;*
> *Made wit with musing weak, heart sick with thought.*

And when Proteus is tempted by the sight of Silvia he employs his craft in wooing her (2.4.210-211)

> *If I can check my erring love, I will;*
> *If not, to compass her I'll use my skill.*

And in the wooing Proteus also uses his wit (2.6.42-43)

> *Love, lend me wings to make my purpose swift,*
> *As thou hast lent me wit to plot this drift.*

Proteus then goes on to try to capture Silvia's affection; he attempts this by sending her letters and gifts (4.4.122; 126-131)

> Jul.: *This is the letter to your ladyship.*
> Sil.: *I will not look upon your master's lines.*
> *I know they are stuffed with protestations*
> *And full of new-found oaths, which he will break*
> *As easily as I do tear his paper.* [Tears the letter.]
> Jul.: *Madam, he sends your ladyship this ring.*

And finally he tries to court her with song (4.2.16-17)

> *Now must we to her window,*
> *And give some evening music to her ear.*

All these attempts by Proteus to woo Silvia fail but they are part of a courtier's standard repertoire as is revealed by Valentine when he instructs the Duke on the new fashions of courting (3.1.89-91)

> *Win her with gifts if she respects not words*
> *Dumb jewels often in their silent kind*
> *More than quick words do move a woman's mind.*

Valentine and Proteus share much in common as lovers. In fact all the lovers including Julia and Lance bear many of the standard symptoms Ficino points out to be seen in the besotted (Ficino, Speech VI, Chpt. 9, p.124)

"For who can conceal Love, whom a wild, ox-like, fixed stare betrays, whom stammering speech reveals, and redness of paleness of face, frequent sighs, shaking of the parts, perpetual complaining, inappropriate praises, sudden indignation, boasting, flirting, petulance, groundless suspicion, and obsequious devotions, all give away?...

So external evidences accompany the internal fire of love".

Speed eloquently makes this same observation of Valentine's comparable behaviours (2.4.126-140) recognizing in his external actions Valentine's internal passion (2.1.31; 34-36)

> *They are all perceived without ye*
> *But you are so without*
> *these follies, that these follies are within you, and shine*
> *through you like the water in a urinal.*

Similarly all the lovers share the blindness that accompanies love (Ficino, Speech VI, Chpt. 10, p.126)

> *"For lovers, blinded by the clouds of love, often accept false things for true, while they think that their beloveds are more beautiful, more intelligent, or better than they are".*

Speed teases Valentine about this (2.1.59-66)

>Spd.: *You never saw her since she was deformed.*
>
>Val.: *How long hath she been deformed?*
>
>Spd.: *Eversince you loved her.*
>
>Val.: *I have loved her ever since I saw her, and still I see her beautiful.*
>
>Spd.: *If you love her, you cannot see her.*
>
>Val.: *Why?*
>
>Spd.: *Because love is blind.*

This same phenomenon occurs with Proteus and he is confused by it, for he doesn't understand what he sees in Silvia that he didn't in Julia (2.4.196)

> *She is fair, and so is Julia that I love*

and vise-versa (5.4.113-114)

> *What is in Silvia's face but I may spy*
> *More fresh in Julia's, with a constant eye?*

as his fancy switches from one to the other.

Proteus, as a lover, behaves very much as the others do but with one particular difference; Proteus acts selfishly.

Proteus and Love's Changeable Nature

Ficino's Commentary establishes that love can be both constant and changeable or more precisely that it has both an immortal and mortal nature. His explanation makes Proteus' behaviour understandable and his sudden shifts explainable. Shakespeare's compressed time line does him no favors in this regard but by understanding Ficino we can better apprehend both Proteus' shift in affection to Silvia and his equally swift shift back to Julia (Ficino, Speech VI, Chpt. 10, p.128-129)

"...in the appetite of men, from the beginnings of life, there is an inextinguishable innate fervor which does not permit the soul to rest, and always forces it to devote itself zealously to some definite thing. The temperaments of men are diverse, and one does not live by a single vow. Whence that continuous ardor of concupiscence, which is natural love, impels some to the study of letters, others to music or painting, others to virtue of conduct, or the religious life, others to honors, some to making money, many to the pleasures of the stomach and of Venus, and others to other things, and also the same man to different things at different ages. <u>And so this fervor is called both immortal and mortal. Immortal because it is never extinguished...Mortal because it does not always concentrate on the same object...It is also called immortal for the reason that a figure once loved is always loved</u>...you always love this same figure fixed forever in your memory, and whenever it presents itself to the eyes of your soul, it burns you with love. <u>For this reason whenever we meet a person whom we used to love, we are shaken</u>...For his presence brings up to the eyes of the soul the figure lying hidden in the mind, and, as if by blowing, <u>rekindles the fires</u> slumbering under the ashes. This is why Love is called immortal. But he is also said to be mortal, for this reason, that although the beloved's features remain fixed forever in the breast, nevertheless they do not present themselves to the eyes of the mind all the time".

It is Proteus' separation from Julia that allows him to forget her in his mind (but not his soul). This allows Proteus to shift his affections to a target of similar virtue; for both Julia and Silvia resonate with the same ideal she holds in his soul (2.4.190-192; 196-199)

> *Or as one nail by strength drives out another,*
> *So the remembrance of my former love*

> *Is by a newer object quite forgotten.*
> *She is fair; and so is Julia that I love –*
> *That I did love, for now my love is thawed,*
> *Which like a waxen image 'gainst a fire*
> *Bears no impression of the thing it was.*

Proteus' shifting passions compromise his reason *"her picture...hath dazzled my reasons light"* (2.4.206-207) but subliminally his soul is still directing him to a virtuous goal – Silvia and Julia are both virtuous. His passions, however, have blinded his reason and they are taking him on the path to selfishness and his own destruction. It is the same situation Lucetta warned Julia of to keep her in check (2.7.21-23)

> *I do not seek to quench your Love's hot fire,*
> *But qualify the fire's extreme rage,*
> *Lest it should burn above the bounds of reason.*

Julia certainly loves Proteus as much as Proteus loves Silvia; she, speaking as Sebastian, clearly states so in the play (4.4.77-80)

> *Because methinks that she loved you as well*
> *As you do love your lady Silvia.*
> *She dreams on him that has forgot her love;*
> *You dote on her that cares not for your love*

but Julia does not let her love burn beyond reason – she does not dote/idolize as Proteus does and she never plots to harm anyone in her pursuit of her beloved. Proteus, on the other hand, has plotted against Valentine and Turio and has done harm against Julia by reducing her to a shadow (Speech II, Chpt. 8, p.55)

"There are two kinds of love: one is simple, the other reciprocal. Simple love is where the beloved does not love the lover. There the lover is completely dead. For he neither lives in himself...nor does he live in the beloved, since he is rejected by him".

Julia has given her soul to Proteus but he has assigned his soul to another (Silvia) so Julia is reduced to a living death, a shadow with no soul (Speech II, Chpt. 8, p.55)

"...*whoever loves, dies. For his attention, oblivious of himself, is always turned to the beloved. If he does not think about himself he certainly does not think in himself. And therefore a soul thus affected does not function in itself, since the special function of the soul is thought itself...Therefore the soul of a lover does not exist in itself because it does not function in itself...it also does not live in itself. He who does not live is dead. Therefore anyone who loves is dead in himself. But at least he lives in another? Certainly*".

Julia speaks of her quasi-existence as "*a shadow*" (4.2.124) and Proteus refers to the deaths of the two lovers he knows: Julia and Valentine (4.2.102; 109). He also understands his own existence as a shadow because Silvia has devoted herself to another (4.2.120-121)

> *For since the substance of your perfect self*
> *Is else devoted, I am but a shadow.*

Valentine best communicates this complex interrelationship between lovers when he laments his banishment (3.1.170-172)

> *And why not death*
> *To die is to be banished from myself,*
> *And Silvia is myself; banished from her*
> *Is self from self.*

Lance is more correct than he knows when he refers to Valentine's banishment as his being "*vanished*" (3.1.214).

These references to death within the confines of love may seem paradoxical but it is the extremity of the soul's commitment that creates the similarity. This is also why lovers are referred to by Ficino as 'murderers and thieves' (Speech VI, Chpt. 10, p.129)

"In addition to these things is the fact that neither animal nor human love can ever exist without hate. Who would not hate one who took his soul away from him?...And so you hate and love beautiful men at the same time; you hate them as <u>thieves and murders</u>; you are also forced to love and revere them as mirrors sparkling with the heavenly glow.

...You would not want to be with this <u>murderer</u> of yourself, but you would not want to live without his blessed sight.

...You cannot live without him, who, with wonderful enticements, <u>steals</u> you from yourself, who claims all of you for himself. You want to flee him who scorches you with his flames. You also want to cling to him, in order that by being very near him who possesses you, you may also be near yourself. You seek yourself outside yourself".

Valentine is the noble lover in the play and according to Ficino this makes him a murderer and a thief and it maybe the reason why Shakespeare assigns Valentine the role of General to the pack of Outlaws who are murderers and thieves in the play (4.1.60). These Outlaws seem extraordinarily impressed by Valentine's ability with words (4.1.33)

Have you the tongues?

This may refer to an ability to speak foreign languages but I believe it refers to a conceit Valentine made earlier in the play (3.1.104-105)

That man that hath a tongue, I say, is no man
If with his tongue he cannot win a woman.

Murderers, thieves, and lovers are all the same in Ficino's work and I believe serve the same purpose in Shakespeare's. For it is in these 'Outlaws' woods' that the lovers are exposed for the thieves and murderers that they are (5.4.43-45)

Prot.: *O'tis the curse of love*
When women cannot love where they're beloved.
Sil.: *When Proteus cannot love where he's beloved.*

The hate that Proteus bears to the object of his love becomes palpable when his tongue fails to move her (5.4.55-58)

Nay, if the gentle spirit of moving words
Can no way change you to a milder form,
I'll woo you like a soldier, at arm's end,
And love you 'gainst the nature of love – force ye.
[Seizes her.]

The violence depicted occurs between the two lovers that can be considered murderers and thieves. Silvia is murderer to Proteus because she has stolen his soul and returned none of his love. Proteus is murder to Julia as he has done likewise to her. The two individuals that can remedy the situation, Valentine and Julia, watch from the wings. Both recognize the coming tragedy for (5.2.7)

love will not be spurred to what it loathes.

Valentine is the correct match for Silvia; her soul is with him and his with her. Their reunion restores them both (5.4.11)

Repair me with thy presence, Silvia.

Proteus' and Julia's relationship is more complex. Julia still yearns for Proteus but he must first remember (Speech VI, Chpt. 11, p.131)

"And if anything escapes the soul through forgetfulness, or lies inert through inactivity or neglect, by diligence in recall and meditation...it restores to the mind what had either perished through forgetfulness, or had grown inactive through laziness".

Proteus must be swept up by the immortal nature of love – that a person once loved is always loved. When Julia faints Proteus' attention is shifted towards her and he begins to remember her (Speech VI, Chpt. 10, p. 128)

"...presence brings up to the eyes of the soul the figure lying hidden in the mind, and, as if by blowing, rekindles the fires slumbering under the ashes".

His soul recognizes Julia's soul and now it is Silvia's image that melts from his memory. His soul is remembering Julia's virtues and wondering what it saw as lacking and as it stares it repairs *"it illuminates them with its own rays and perfects them"* (Speech VI, Chpt. 10, p.130). This process restores Julia to Proteus. They once more share each other's souls – seeing each other in each other. The murderers and thieves are appropriately matched each possessing and caring for the other's soul (looking to the good of the other) so that justice can prevail and pardons can be issued all around.

Rediscovering Julia

Val.: *And that my love may appear plain and free,*
　　　All that was mine in Silvia I give thee.

Jul.: *O me unhappy!* [Faints]

These verses (5.4.82-83) have been read in two ways. Because Shakespeare based the play partly on the story of 'Titus and Gisippus' many critics make the assumption that since this work involved the gifting of a woman from one friend to another that this was also Shakespeare's intention. Others read the lines as 'all that was my love in Silvia I give thee' meaning Valentine restores Proteus to the same level of trust and friendship as he affords to Silvia.

I believe both interpretations contribute something. Shakespeare knew his source material. He knew the public had a memory of these works and I believe he played on their expectations of an exchange in order to deceive the audience, just for a moment, and in much the same way as he deceives Julia in the play. I believe Valentine's only intention is to communicate to Proteus that he is restored in his eyes. Valentine clearly intends no offer of Silvia to Proteus <u>but</u> at the same time Shakespeare has carefully worded the phrase to be misunderstood or misheard by Julia who is on the stage but off to one side. It's Julia's reaction to the partial text, to the phrase *"...Silvia I give thee"* that causes her to faint and to be discovered and in fact recovered in Proteus' affections.

Julia hears the phrase through the filter of her own worst fears. She has witnessed Proteus betray her repeatedly since she has come to Verona and her worst fear is that he will be successful in his pursuit of Silvia; when she hears the words *"...Silvia I give thee"* her world comes crashing down. But, as in all comedies, the audience knows more than Julia. We can interpret the lines based on what we know of Valentine and Silvia's love, information not privy to Julia. We know Valentine lives through Silvia and would never betray or abandon her (3.1.182-184)

She is my essence, and I leave (cease) *to be*
If I be not by her fair influence
Fostered, illuminated, cherished, kept alive.

Julia's fainting allows the play to shift its focus away from Proteus' bad behaviour back to his more compassionate side (5.4.84)

Look to the boy.

The disguise Julia is wearing allows his soul to recognize Julia before he does. The fainting allows for some sympathetic concern to be expressed prior to realizing who Sebastian is and before recognizing what ordeals he has put Julia through. Julia has held on to Proteus throughout the play and through all the trials. She has held on to the 'changing Proteus' and just as in Ovid's myth Proteus speaks oracally when held and not released (5.4.109-111)

were man
But constant he were perfect. That one error
Fills him with faults.

And with this true revelation we know he understands that to be guided by the 'divine light' is now his constant goal. For love must be just to be true; each caring for the other as they would themselves. True equality in the shared soul requires balance between the physical and the spiritual, the innate and the infused, the twin lights that govern the one soul. Perfection arising from the unchangeable infused soul directing the changeable innate flesh.

Conclusion

Many regard *The Two Gentlemen of Verona* as a clumsy early work by Shakespeare. I could not disagree more. The play reflects a deep familiarity with Plato and more particularly with Ficino's commentary on Plato. Shakespeare adeptly integrates Aristophanes' fable of the fall of man into the structure of his play. The play itself is full of parallels, echoes, and elaborations on themes of love and it broadly fleshes out its points of view. These strong internal structures add a unity and coherence to the play and make it into a very tight and balanced work [3].

Realizing that the play does not belong to the same friendship tradition that was mined as its source material is the first step to recognizing what the play is about. Aristophanes' version of the 'fall of man' and forgiveness by love is comparable to the parable of the Prodigal son and both act as a structural metaphor for the play. In Aristophanes the divided man longs to regain his integrity and in Shakespeare's tale it is Julia, the same Julia who reassembles Proteus' letters, who possesses the power to reassemble Proteus himself.

Footnotes

[1] All underlining in quoted passages is done for emphasis only and is not part of the original text.

[2] There is a pattern emerging in Shakespeare's works – he returns to Ficino or more particularly to specific stories within Ficino to construct metaphorical themes for certain of his plays – one story for one play.

Each play appears to draw its primary metaphor from a single speech found in Ficino's *Commentary of Plato's Symposium on Love*. I have found three such plays that appear to meet this criterion.

a) Pausanius' speech (Ficino, Speech II, Chpt. 7-9) appears to provide the central metaphor of the heavenly and vulgar Venuses that is pivotal to understanding Shakespeare's *All's Well That Ends Well*. This is examined in detail in my essay 'Unsatisfied Longing in *All's Well That Ends Well*' found in my book *Presence in Absence* (2010).

b) Phadrus' speech (Speech I, Chpt. 3) on the birth of love from chaos I believe is integral in understanding *King Lear,* a story founded in chaos and where love is used as a weapon until its final scene. This idea is explored in the essay 'King Lear and the Blinding of Cupid' found in my book *In Sheep's Clothing* (2008).

c) Aristophanes' speech (Speech IV, Chpt. 1-5) concerning the twin lights of the soul is explored in this present essay and I believe is central to appreciating *The Two Gentlemen of Verona*.

The speeches provide a focus for philosophical debate. They provide Shakespeare with a concept that can be explored in many ways but which still revolve around a central idea; this restricts his play and helps to define its limits. Flexible and yet restrictive; the metaphor functions as a program for the writing of specific plays.

[3] Without labouring the point *The Two Gentlemen of Verona* is full of parallels, echoes, and elaborations that create a unity and coherence to the play and make it a tightly balanced work. Some examples of these are:

The play begins with Proteus showing the physical symptoms of love, these symptoms we will later see displayed by both Valentine and Lance.

Proteus' love for Julia is opposed by his family as is Valentine's love for Silvia.

Proteus' father sends Proteus away from Julia and the Duke banishes Valentine from Silvia.

Proteus, Valentine, and Julia all claim to be metamorphosed by love.

Julia loves Proteus as Proteus loves Silvia but Proteus cares not for Julia as Silvia cares not for Proteus. At a midpoint in the play the Julia-Proteus couple is physically in each other's presence but spiritually separated from each other while the Silvia-Valentine couple are physically but not spiritually separated.

Lance's commitment to his dog throughout the play mimics Julia's commitment to Proteus; the dog and Proteus both being selfish beasts.

Julia at the beginning of the play and Silvia near the end of the play both tear up letters sent to them from Proteus.

Julia, Silvia, Valentine and Proteus at one point in the play all present themselves as 'shadows' of their former selves.

Lance's family and Lance himself display the emotional toll that the others must be feeling due to the separations they must undergo from their loved ones in the play.

Proteus trusts Julia/Sebastian to court Silvia as Valentine trusts Proteus with his secrets. Both have in essence placed their trust in a fox set among lambs.

The Outlaw (Murderers and thieves) scene is placed to correspond to the point where the lovers are most mismatched – where the object of their love does not return their love. In this scene Proteus chooses to strike out with hate while Julia chooses not to hate, but rather to forgive.

This type of textual interconnectedness allows for much variation on a theme and also gives the play a strong introspective structure that isolates it and helps it to form its own little world; one we are privileged to look upon.

Bibliography

1) *The Two Gentlemen of Verona*, W. Shakespeare, edited by William C. Carroll, The Arden Shakespeare, Third Series, 2005.
2) *The Nicomachean Ethics*, Aristotle, transl. H. Rackham, The Loeb Classical Library, 1956.
3) *Commentary on Plato's Symposium on Love*, Marsilio Ficino, translated by Sears Jayne, Spring Publications Inc., 1985.
4) *The Two Gentlemen of Verona as Burlesque*, William Rossky, English Literary Renaissance, 12, 1982, p.210-219.
5) *The French Academie* (1586), P. de la Primandaye, Georg Olms Verlag, 1972.

Twelfth Night: **No Darkness**

Introduction

Twelfth Night is a comic exploration of ideas related to anarchy and order. It accomplishes this by setting its action on the last day of the Christmas season, Twelfth Night, which was also the Day of Epiphany, a religious holiday marking the revelation of Christ. Because of this conjuncture Twelfth Night functioned as a meeting place between pagan festivities and religious tradition. Its pagan roots were reflected in all forms of merry-making and mummery (the wearing of disguises) as well as in the election of a Mock King, the Lord of Misrule, who presided over the revels. It was a time when convention was overturned and traditional authority gave way to the anarchic spirit of Saturnalia (*Twelfth Night*, Arden edition, 3rd series, Introduction, *Around Twelfth Night*, p. 17-24). The Day of Epiphany was, however, a much more modest affair celebrating the presence of God through Christ in the world; as such Twelfth Night marked the intersection of the carnivalesque with the abstinent; where a playful anarchy threatened to corrupt order.

In Shakespeare's first act the forces of anarchy begin to exercise control over the plot and his very proper main characters, Orsino and Olivia. Anarchy is introduced in the form of love (1.1.1) *"If music be the food of love, play on"*. Love overthrows Orsino's reason with his passions. Orsino seeks love's excess and proves no longer to be the prudent leader of Illyria but rather a 'fool for love' whose judgment is consumed by his desires (1.1.21-22). Olivia, on the other hand, in keeping with the spirit of the religious holiday cloisters herself until she too is smitten with an irrepressible and slightly deluded love for a disguised bisexual, Viola/Cesario.

Disguises, deceptions, and mistaken identities each play their part as they unravel the order of Illyria and introduce mayhem. Anarchy reigns as individuals are at a loss to determine what is genuine and what is not, both in peoples' appearances and in their actions. The play becomes a comic house of mirrors but with a deeply conceived philosophical foundation. It is the purpose of this essay to demonstrate that Bruno's 'philosophy of the ass' as set out in his works, *The Cabala of Pegasus* (*Cabala del cavallo pegaseo,* 1585), *The Nolan's Cillenican Ass* (*A l'asino cillenico del nolano,* 1585), and *The Expulsion of the Triumphant Beast* (*Lo spaccio della bestia trionfante,* 1584), forms a substratum of ideas that are resonant throughout Shakespeare's play and that helps to inform his work.

Delusion, Disguise and Deception

Delusion is one of our greatest weaknesses and we all can be easily deceived. Much of our reasoning depends on reliable input to our senses but if that input is faulty then so is the output (our actions). Decisions made on bad information leads us into error. The Elizabethans were acutely aware of this and subsequently concerned over the role imagination played on our faculty of Reason (W. Rossky, *Imagination in the English Renaissance*).

Imagination or Phantasy, words they used interchangeably, was seen as a key faculty in the mind. All sensory information received was pooled in the Common Sense which then informed the Phantasy where it was converted into images that the higher faculties (Understanding and Reason) could meditate upon. This idea can be traced to Aristotle's *Metaphysics* where he stated *"There is nothing in the intellect that was not first in the senses"* and a sentiment he rephrased as *"To think was to speculate with images"* (*De Anima,* Book III, Chapt. 3). Because the

Phantasy was a gateway to the higher faculties it was critical that it be reliable for the faculty of Reason could only be as accurate as the images presented to it.

The more conservative elements of society, like the Puritans, held the Phantasy in disrepute; they felt it could falsify information. It was suspect because of its close association with the senses which were tied to the flesh and therefore subject to 'the sins of the flesh'. Phantasy, they felt, could be disproportionately attracted to this physical world and give more importance to the body's sensual desires. Worse still the Phantasy was an 'active faculty' so it was capable of building onto the information it received. The general fear was that the Phantasy, or more precisely its images, could disproportionately stimulate the passions to override reason and thereby lead to irrational behaviour.

This understanding of the Phantasy is echoed in *Twelfth Night* in its very first scene. It is in fact the Phantasy's active capacity of unlimited creativity that is highlighted (1.1.14-15)

> *So full of shapes is fancy*
> *That it alone is high fantastical.*

This much feared delusional effect of the Phantasy was even more exaggerated when the person was in love. This effect is outlined in the work of Ficino written in 1482 and widely available (*Commentary on Plato's Symposium on Love*, Speech VI, Chapt. 10, p.126)

"*For lovers, blinded by clouds of love, often accept false things for true, while they think that their beloveds are more beautiful, more intelligent, or better than they are*".

This sentiment is confirmed by Olivia (1.5.295-296) when smitten by Viola/Cesario

> *I do I know not what, and fear to find*
> *Mine eye too great a flatter for my mind.*

Delusion by our own minds (self-delusion) is only one danger we face in trying to ascertain the truth about our world; we also are subject to deception by others. This deception can be intentional, such as that practiced by Toby on Malvolio, or it can be unintentional, such as Viola's unwitting seduction of Olivia. In either case actions are set in motion based on information that is faulty. These actions, in turn, though genuine do not reflect the true natures of the persons performing them. The old adage *"You shall know them by their fruits"* (Matt. 7:16) is rendered meaningless. Malvolio's actions are those of a mad man but Malvolio's motives are to act in a way he believes his beloved has requested. He is acting sanely but following insane orders. The same is true of Olivia; she is in fact courting another woman but this is not true to her intensions nor reflective of her true nature; she is not a lesbian. Viola's disguise, adopted for one purpose, is having unintentional consequences (2.2.27)

Disguise, I see thou art a wickedness.

This slice of Illyria is presented as a place where the actions of others cannot be seen as indicative of their true natures or representative of the people they are. Sebastian, a newcomer, cannot make any sense of the way he is treated (4.1.59-60)

How runs the stream?

Or I am mad or else this is a dream

for as in a dream, logic does not seem to apply.

In *Twelfth Night* senses are subject to delusion and actions are severed from their intent so we are left only with people's words to inform us. But this too proves fruitless. Words we find are too imprecise, too unlimited, too coloured by human assumptions and emotions to effectively reveal reality. Feste speaks of this with Viola (3.1.19-24)

Feste*: But indeed words*

    are very rascals, since bonds disgraced them.

> Viola: *Thy reason, man?*
>
> Feste: *Troth sir, I can yield you none without words, and words are grown so false I am loath to prove reason with them.*

and again (3.1.11-13)

> *A sentence is but*
> *a cheverel glove to a good wit; how quickly the wrong*
> *side may be turned outward.*

Words are in fact even less dependable than actions for they are so easy to give (2.4.117-118)

> *Our shows are more than will*
> *for still we prove*
> *Much in our vows, but little in our love.*

The characters are at a loss seeking a match between the external appearance of a thing or action and its truthful reality. We are forewarned of the importance of this concept when Viola compliments the sea captain on both his appearance and his nature (1.2.45-48)

> *...nature with a beauteous wall*
> *Doth oft close in pollution, yet of thee*
> *I will believe thou hast a mind that suits*
> *With this thy fair and outward character.*

Characters are seeking the simple assurance of *"That that is is"* (4.2.14-15) but find themselves only being left with the wish *"O say so, and so be"* (4.1.64).

Every character is made into a fool or ass by their own self delusion or by other people's deceptions or through mistaken identity. Because of their limited grasp of the truth the characters are set adrift in waters that are difficult to navigate; a place where people's words, actions and feelings are all suspect and only give them a glimpse of reality.

We Are All Asses

The idea that everyone is a fool is introduced by Feste when he comes upon Sir Toby and Sir Andrew; he asks them (2.3.15-16)

Did you never see the

picture of 'we three'?

They respond with *"welcome, ass"*, showing they are aware of the concept. The picture he refers to was of an image of two asses with a caption reading 'we three'. The implication being that whoever was viewing the picture was the third ass. It was a universal acknowledgement that we are all asses or fools, a theme in keeping with the sentiments of the play.

Many characters are referred to directly as asses such as Sir Andrew Aguecheek (5.1.202-203)

An ass-head and a coxcomb and

a knave, a thin-faced knave, a gull

and Malvolio (2.3.143)

an affectioned ass

or indirectly as again Malvolio with the comment *"Go shake your ears"* or Feste when he adopts the persona of Sir Topas (Top Ass) the curate.

These references all allude to the universal nature of foolery (3.1.37-38)

Foolery, sir, does walk about the orb like the sun,

it shines everywhere

and therein lies one of the keys to understanding the philosophical basis behind *Twelfth Night*.

The Philosophy of the Ass

For Giordano Bruno, one of the most cutting edge philosophers of the sixteenth century, the humble ass represented the vehicle for divine revelation i.e. epiphany. Bruno used the ass as his symbol for 'saintly asininity' a concept he borrowed from Nicholas of Cusa (1401-1464) which Nicholas termed as 'learned ignorance' [1]. It stemmed from his belief that humans were condemned to ignorance in that we could not know things precisely. By this he did not mean that we could not know anything but merely that our knowledge had to be tempered with uncertainty (*Nicholas of Cusa On Learned Ignorance*, Book 1, Chapt. 2, sec.8)

"I show at the outset that learned ignorance has its basis in the fact that the precise truth is inapprehensible".

It was only from this point of ignorance that learning could truly begin. He founded his philosophy on his understanding of Socrates. He felt Socrates to be wise precisely because he knew that he did not know (ibid., Book 1, Chapt. 1, sec. 4)

"Socrates seemed to himself to know nothing except that he did not know.

For a man...The more he knows that he is unknowing, the more learned he will be".

In *Twelfth Night* Feste reiterates this comment (1.5.31-32)

> *Those wits that think they have thee do very oft prove*
> *fools, and I that am sure I lack thee may pass for a wise*
> *man*

but it is the play itself that is infused with the kind of uncertainty Nicholas speaks of for here much is not what it seems. The outward appearance is at odds with its internal essence, for example, Viola's confession (3.1.139) "*I am not what I am*", Feste's exasperated plea (4.1.8) "*nothing that is so is so*", Orsino's paradoxical assessment (5.1.213) "*A natural perspective, that is and is not*", and finally Sebastian's suspicion that things are not quite right in Illyria (4.3.20-21) "*There's something in't / That is deceivable*".

It is this atmosphere of uncertainty which is in keeping with Nicholas' philosophy that allows *Twelfth Night* to act as an allegory for both his and Bruno's philosophies. To be ignorant meant to be skeptical of what you sense/perceive and of the motives you attribute to any actions. It was to let your mind exist in a state of possibility.

For Nicholas the great Trinity (God, Spirit, Christ) was expressed through the ideas of unlimited possibility (God) coming into actuality (Christ) through motion/action (Spirit). Nicholas believed God was Oneness, the All. All that was, all that is, and all that could be, existed in this Oneness (ibid., Book 1, Chapt. 22, sec. 67)

"God is the enfolding of all things, even of contradictories"
and again (ibid.,Book 1, Chapt. 24, sec. 75)

"for in His simplicity He enfolds the totality of things".

Physical creation was an unfolding of this infinite possibility in a finite way. Creation occurred through a contraction of the infinite i.e. a lessening of possibility. In Nicholas' philosophy *"oneness precedes otherness"* (ibid., Book II, Chapt. 3, sec. 107) in the sense that a 'universal oneness that contains all' precedes any distinct form that arises from that oneness. Nicholas felt (ibid., Book II, Chapt. 3, sec. 107) *"identity precedes difference, equality precedes inequality"* i.e. the universal oneness always precedes any discrimination from this universal. *Twelfth Night* is imbued with the spirit of this philosophy: what Bruno has enfolded from Nicholas, Shakespeare has unfolded in *Twelfth Night*. The bisexual Viola/Cesario with her same sex/heterosexual relationships creates an atmosphere of mutability; she is an ambiguous figure representing the oneness of sex before it unfolds into Viola, the female, and Sebastian, the male. Her ambiguous bisexual relationships precede her traditional relationship with Orsino. The less defined universals precede the more specific versions derived from that universal.

But there is more to the 'ass philosophy' than just learned ignorance and the unfolding of the universal for Bruno has also merged Nicholas of Cusa's philosophy with that of Jewish Kabbalah. He did this in his work *Cabala del cavallo pegaseo* (*The Cabala of Pegasus*) published in England (1585), although he had it stamped Parigi (Paris). Bruno felt that new insights could be derived from the merging of wisdom and foolishness, knowledge and ignorance. He defined this aspect of his philosophy the 'coincidence of contraries' or the 'coincidence of opposites'. He derived this concept by expanding on Nicholas' idea 'that God enfolds all things, even contraries into a oneness' with Kabbalah's practice of setting opposing forces into a dynamic equilibrium with a third connecting and balancing force.

The calendrical event, Twelfth Night, referred to a time when the carnivalesque met with sober reflection. In terms of Bruno's philosophy it represented the coincidence of opposites and therefore a time rife with the possibility of new insights.

Appended to Bruno's *The Cabala of Pegasus* is a smaller essay *A l'asino cillenico del nolano* (*The Nolan's Cillenican Ass*). This smaller work tells the story of an Ass who has passed through various lives in various forms and the troubles he encounters when he tries to enter the Pythagorean Academy (*The Cabala of Pegasus, The Nolan's Cillenican Ass*, p. 86)

"*Although I am an ass in form at present, I may have been and may yet be in form a great man; and although you are a man, you may have been and may yet be a great ass, according to what will seem expedient to the distributor of clothes and abodes, and the dispatcher of transmigrant souls*".

In this work Bruno affirmed his Pythagorean beliefs (*The Cabala of Pegasus*, p. 55-56, p.63)

"Fate treats the asinine soul no differently than the human, and the spirit that constitutes those so-called animals than what is found in all things".

"So you maintain steadfastly that the soul of the human is no different in substance than that of the beast".

Bruno's dialogue reiterated and extended the thoughts of Plotinus (Plotinus, *Enneads* (4:8))

"all souls are derived from the same principle from which the universal Soul also is derived".

Bruno's essay is incredibly egalitarian and concludes with the god Mercury assisting the Ass in gaining admittance to the academy. Mercury assures the Ass (*The Cabala of Pegasus, The Nolan's Cillenican Ass*, p. 90)

"You may enter and reside anywhere, without anyone able to bar the door to you or to give any sort of insult or impediment...mix with everyone; discourse with everyone; fraternize, unite, and identify with everyone; rule over everyone; be everything".

In *Twelfth Night* there is a democratizing undercurrent in the story. We see this with the Viola and Sebastian plot lines. Though they are strangers to the land of Illyria both marry far above their station; what position they hold in Messaline we are never really made aware of aside from a few veiled comments that they behave like gentlemen and are employed beneath their station (1.5.270-271). Malvolio, too, is chaffing at the bit to rise above his current position. His 'luck rich' dreams of being given status (marrying into status) make him an easy dupe for Maria and Toby's scheme but it's his desire to ascend that reveals a deeper societal urge for change to the current status quo. Malvolio, though a servant, believes his true nature is to be above his present circumstances.

Bruno's egalitarian influence resonates in Malvolio's interaction with the fool (dressed as Sir Topas). In Bruno's *The Cabala of Pegasus* three terms are used interchangeably; these are asininity–madness–and ignorance. Bruno uses these terms as synonyms (*The Cabala of Pegasus*, First Dialogue, p. 34, p.51)

> *"Have you never heard that insanity, ignorance, and asininity of this world are wisdom, doctrine, and divinity in the other"*

and *"O holy ignorance, O divine insanity, O superhuman asininity!"*

These three terms come together when the fool disguised as Sir Topas (Top Ass) meets with Malvolio (the madman). The ass is there to 'cure' the madman who has been kept in literal darkness (ignorance).

The fool is a transitive character. He freely moves through society and takes liberties with all classes. He calls Olivia, the countess, a fool (1.5.66-68), he dresses up as his betters e.g. Sir Topas the curate, and is insolent to Count Orsino (2.4.73-78). The immunity granted him as a fool (*an allowed fool* (1.5.90)) permits him to speak the truth. He is the most democratic of characters and offers the secret of social mobility to Malvolio, a man who is the most class conscious of any in the play. Malvolio carefully observes both time and place in his behaviours and in the behaviours of others *"confine yourself within the modest limits of order"* (1.3.7-8). The fool offers a type of advice that can take Malvolio out of both literal and intellectual darkness if he can but solve the riddle (4.2.42-43)

> *I say there is no darkness*
> *but ignorance.*

When the fool tests Malvolio's madness he does so by asking his opinion concerning Pythagoras' idea of the transmigration of souls, a concept Malvolio dismisses (4.2.49-58)

> Feste: *What is the opinion of Pythagoras concerning*
> *wildfowl?*

Mal.: *That the soul of our grandam might haply inhabit a bird.*

Feste: *What think'st thou of his opinion?*

Mal.: *I think nobly of the soul, and no way approve his opinion.*

Feste: *Fare thee well. Remain thou still in darkness. Thou shalt hold th'opinion of Pythagoras ere I will allow of thy wits.*

If Malvolio could believe in the transmigration of the soul then he could believe in the equality of all souls. He could then believe that the soul of a Count is no different than his soul or for that matter no different than the soul of an ass. This revelation could free him of his belief that the classes are divinely ordained. He could come to understand that the dreams he normally represses of class mobility could on some level be attainable at least through hard work and merit.

The cruel trick done to him by Toby and Maria made him reveal his ambitions but his public humiliation will undoubtedly kill any further aspirations. The revelation offered Malvolio by the fool was genuine. Such a Pythagorean belief would take him out of darkness, it would give him hope that all are created equal but it does come with a cost. The chance for ascendancy is linked to empathy. If you believe all souls are the same you must treat everyone with equal respect, duke or fool. Until Malvolio can hold such an opinion he will remain in darkness.

The Transmigration Theme

I believe that Shakespeare approaches his plays in much the same way as he approaches his sonnets. Just as key words and ideas repeat throughout the stanzas of a sonnet so too do they in the various acts making up his play. Ideas introduced early in the play will repeat as variations on a theme, they will be explored and elaborated on throughout the rest of the work.

In the case of *Twelfth Night* Shakespeare introduces the idea or concept of transmigration or transformation very early on; he does it by having Orsino allude to the story of Actaeon, a man who was transformed into a stag and then hunted by his own dogs (1.1.18; 20-22)

> *O, when mine eyes did see Olivia first*
> *That instant was I turned into a hart,*
> *And my desires, like fell and cruel hounds,*
> *E'er since pursue me.*

Orsino sees himself first transformed and then plagued by his desires. Transformation, is of itself, not an uncommon theme in a love story but in this play the theme is unusually literal. Viola/Cesario is a transitive character, literally a woman disguised as a boy but this boy, in turn, is also transformative (1.5.152-155)

> *Not yet old enough for a man, nor young*
> *enough for a boy, as a squash is before 'tis a peascod,*
> *or a codling when 'tis almost an apple. 'Tis with him in*
> *standing water between boy and man.*

This transformative nature is also seen in the material that people wear (2.4.74-75)

> *the/tailor make thy doublet of changeable taffeta, for thy*
> *mind is very opal.*

Taffeta is a silk that appears different colours when seen from different angles and opal is a gem stone that again takes on different hues when seen from various angles or in different light.

All these transitions inform the scene between Feste and Malvolio where Feste tries to get Malvolio to admit to the possibility of transmigration of souls (4.2.49-58) from one body to another.

These transformative possibilities are suggestive of the idea that the constant soul lies hidden beneath a changeable body or skin. Orsino can love Viola/Cesario as a woman even though he has never seen her as such because he is aware of her devotion and constancy in his service. He loves her essence; her soul. Ficino spoke of this in his description of the soul (*Commentary on Plato's Symposium on Love*, Speech IV, Chapt. 3, p. 75)

"Therefore Man is the soul alone; the body is merely a work an instrument of Man...therefore the soul can take the name of Man as proper to itself, independent of the mass of the body.

Since each of us throughout our entire life is called "Man", at any age, then surely this name seems to signify something that remains fixed. The body is perpetually in flux, changed by growing and shrinking...The soul always remains the same".

This can also be said of Antonio, he knows Sebastian, the man, through his actions, he trusts him. The false name Sebastian used, *Roderigo* (2.1.16), is irrelevant to their relationship for he admires the essence of the man.

The idea of a soul or a self that was distinct from the 'skin it was in' was understood as a commonplace by the characters in the play for it underlies Malvolio's caution to Toby (2.3.95-97)

If you
can separate yourself and your misdemeanours, you
are welcome to the house

and Toby also speaks of this separation of body and soul (3.4.231)

Souls and bodies hath he divorced three.

The self was seen as distinct from one's actions and one's body.

The Self

Bruno's philosophy does not just help us see an alternative to the rigid class system but it also affords an understanding of the self. The psychologist Rollo May (*Psychology and the Human Dilemma*, p. 58) focused on Bruno's fierce self-assertion and individualism when he discussed Bruno's idea of Creation as a series of concentric circles with the self at the center. This pre-modern belief had its roots in Aristotle and the fact that 'all we know comes first from our senses'. All of creation, all that we know, our version of the world is unique to ourselves. In any crowd of people there are hundreds of unique worlds each centered on the individual self. Bruno's idea of creation dovetailed nicely with his view of the universe as one that was full of infinite worlds just like our own. A universe which placed no greater significance on our world than it did on any other (*De l'infinito universo e mondi*, On the Infinite Universe and Worlds, 1580). Bear in mind Bruno was espousing these sacrilegious ideas at a time when the orthodox opinion was that our world was the only inhabited world and that it was at the center of a finite universe bound by celestial spheres. Bruno's version of the self was egalitarian with each self at the center of their own little world and each world of no greater or lesser significance than the other worlds around them. This view was at odds with a rigid hierarchy where everyone was in their place and every place was assigned a rank and that the resulting 'chain of being' was ordained by God.

Malvolio is a strong believer in this 'chain of being', in the idea of hierarchy (2.5.50-51)

> – *telling them I know*
>
> *my place, as I would they should do theirs*

and he also knows he is rightfully excluded from the elite. He believes in a class system but he also believes he is superior to others and that his current position as house steward is below his proper place.

Unfortunately a rise in rank necessitates a violation to the rules of hierarchy. He is caught in a maddening paradox. Malvolio's inflated 'sense of self' psychologically chips away at this rigid class system and allows him to daydream of advancement at least by marriage. The 'sense of self' and various understandings of what 'self' is dominate the different storylines and in fact drive the story engine for much of the play.

Twelfth Night is on its surface a love story, but it is modeled on the Ficinian idea of love; that love was the death of self. We get this sense early on in the play with the spate of deaths; fathers, brothers, and twins dying; all forms of a loss of self. This theme is reinforced with the three love stories; Orsino's with Olivia; Olivia's with Cesario/Viola and Viola's/Cesario with Orsino. All three represent a type of love that is not reciprocated; a type of love Ficino felt was the equivalent to death (*Commentary on Plato's Symposium on Love*, Speech II, Chapt. 8, p. 55)

"There are two kinds of love: one is simple, the other reciprocal. Simple love is where the beloved does not love the lover. There the lover is completely dead. For he neither lives in himself...nor does he live in the beloved, since he is rejected by him.

...whoever loves dies. For his attention, oblivious of himself, is always turned to the beloved. If he does not think about himself he certainly does not think in himself. And therefore a soul thus affected does not function in itself, since the special function of the soul is thought itself...Therefore the soul of a lover does not exist in itself because it does not function in itself...it also does not live in itself. He who does not live is dead".

This sad aspect of love is revealed when Viola tells Orsino a story about the death of 'his' sister from unconfessed, and therefore unrequited, love (2.4.119) *"But died thy sister of her love, my boy?"*. The unspoken answer to this question is 'yes she will die if she cannot express her love'. It is also a subtext to the exchange between Viola and Olivia when Olivia says of Orsino (1.5.254) *"I cannot love him"*. Viola points out that he cannot accept this answer for his master (1.5.256-259)

> *If I did love you in my master's flame,*
> *With such a suffering, such a deadly life,*
> *In your denial I would find no sense,*
> *I would not understand it.*

Orsino is not thinking in himself, he exists in that Schrodinger state of 'deathly life' neither fully alive nor dead. In love you care about the beloved more than your own self (5.1.129)

> *To do you rest a thousand deaths would die.*

But love can also preserve the self by finding a home in another (ibid., Speech II, Chpt. 8)

> *There is also that fact that the lover engraves the figure of the beloved on his own soul. And so the soul of the lover becomes a mirror in which the image of the beloved is reflected. For that reason, when the beloved recognizes himself in the lover, he is forced to love him.*

This is what happens in reciprocal love, each self preserves and protects the other.

The theme of 'the self' is also present in Shakespeare's use of twins. When the twins are separated self is physically divided from self. A bereaved Viola psychologically restores her lost other self, her brother, by dressing as him. She does so until Sebastian is physically restored to her at the end of the play.

Shakespeare's choice of male/female twins is inspired because it so nicely ties in with the idea that the soul is an egalitarian entity independent of its packaging, an idea inherent in the Pythagorean soul. *Twelfth Night* passively argues that Viola is the same person whether she be Viola or Cesario, female or male and Orsino has no more trouble accepting her as a wife than he does confiding in him as a friend. Viola's true essence is defined by her loyalty, her kindness, and her cleverness - all traits that transcend any particular sexual identity.

Knowledge of self is often gained through trials and in *Twelfth Night* this is true for all the characters. Viola must court another woman for the man she herself loves, Olivia must persevere through continued rejection, Malvolio must endure humiliation, and Andrew is exploited as a gull by his supposed friend Toby. Adversity often teaches us more about ourselves than contentment and in addition to this Feste reveals that we often learn more about ourselves from those we count as enemies than from those we consider our friends (5.1.9-11; 14-18)

>Ors: *How dost thou, my good fellow?*
>Feste: *Truly, sir, the better for my foes, and the worse for my friends.*
>Ors: *How can that be?*
>Feste: *Marry, sir, they praise me and make an ass of me. Now my foes tell me plainly I am an ass, so that by my foes sir, I profit in the knowledge of myself, and by my friends I am abused.*

Not only is this idea that 'our enemies are our friends' in keeping with Bruno's philosophy of coincident opposites but it also proves true in the play. Feste (Malvolio's enemy) gives good advice to Malvolio that could offer him both the hope of bettering himself as well as providing him with a blueprint to his improvement through empathy. Viola's enemies, Toby and Sir Andrew, end up revealing Sebastian's presence and by so doing calm an escalating situation by providing the opportunity Viola needs to reveal her female identity.

Knowing oneself and recognizing the true self of others is key to whether the play is a comedy or tragedy for the characters involved. Orsino is quick to recognize his true love, and his reflected self, in Viola.

Olivia finds reciprocal love in Sebastian. Malvolio is forced to see what everyone knows about him (1.5.86)

> *O, you are sick of self-love.*

and (2.3.146-147)

> *it is his grounds of faith that all that*
> *look on him love him.*

Malvolio lacks empathy for others; his self-love is reflected in his self-importance. His humiliation could be his epiphany, it could awaken his self-knowledge. An empathetic Malvolio, with a humbled spirit, could be a respected leader. He could still *"achieve greatness"* but his dream of having it *"thrust upon"* him is over. Malvolio must decide whether to believe he is still better than everyone else or that he is the same as everyone else, his happy ending depends on his choice.

Rounding out the cast are Sir Andrew and Sir Toby. Sir Andrew is an innocent badly used by Toby. Andrew is what might be referred to as a 'fool natural' as opposed to Feste who is a 'fool professional', but Andrew does not lack self awareness, he knows of his shortcomings (1.3.81-84)

> *Methinks sometimes I have no*
> *more wit than a Christian...*
> *I am a great eater of beef, and I believe that does harm*
> *to my wit.*

and (2.5.79)

> *I knew 'twas I, for many do call me fool.*

If Andrew did harbour any doubt as to his foolishness by the end of the play it is removed as Toby reveals himself to be no friend of Andrew's and bluntly calls him an *"ass-head"* and *"a gull"* (5.1.202-203).

Sir Toby is an entirely self-centered creation. Although Bruno's philosophy speaks of a world centered on the self, as an honest reflection of how we come to know the world, he was in no way promoting selfishness. Toby, however, exists only for Toby. He exploits his cousin Olivia and is generally disrespectful of her wishes. He exploits Sir Andrew as his personal purse and he abuses others in the play for his own personal amusement. Toby knows no limits or boundaries (1.3.9-10)

I'll confine myself no finer than I / am.

Not only is Toby self-centered but he also lacks self awareness. Toby, the drunken rogue, condemns Dick Surgeon for inconveniencing him by complaining (5.1.197)

I hate a drunken rogue.

So a story filled with deception, disguise and mistaken identity is not surprisingly a story about the self and the search for what is genuine amid all these projections. Olivia gives one of the best pieces of advice in the entire play when she tells Viola/Cesario to (5.1.145)

Be that thou knowst thou art.

Self-knowledge and self acceptance are the foundation for the soul and also the only way to navigate in a world of ambiguous truths.

A World of Constant Change

Bruno's 'philosophy of the ass' can be visualized as a cycle or a wheel that reflects humanity's transition from a natural world to one of technology and culture. He considered this transition to occur through a series of oscillations between the actions of positive and negative asses.

Positive asses he saw as taking control. They lived in an action based world and employed their intellect and bodies to do the hard work required for the development of both knowledge and civilization. Negative asses he felt were the upholders of religious myth using it as a brake on the development of knowledge. He saw them as the gangrene of stasis that kills any advancement.

Bruno conceived of a wheel of metamorphosis where the ass occupied the topmost position (divine inspiration, humility, hard work) and humans occupied the bottom position (ignorance, superstition, religion). Man ascended by hard work and humility and descended through arrogance and ignorance; positive asses ascending, negative asses descending.

This dynamic view was in-keeping with his overall philosophy of the 'coincidence of opposites' (*Giordano Bruno and the Logic of Coincidence*, by Antonio Calcagno). A philosophy that held the belief that contraries convert to one another; that they occupied opposite poles of the same circle. The opposites stand in a dynamic relationship to one another; as you move round the circle one contrary becomes its opposite (e.g. hot becomes cold then cold becomes hot). There is no resting place. Both extremes are always present in any given property hence the coincidence of opposites. This circular conceit is true of stasis and development; ignorance and enlightenment; virtue and sin (1.5.44-45)

Virtue that transgresses is but patched with
sin, and sin that amends is but patched with virtue.

In Bruno's work *Lo spaccio della bestia trionfante* (*The Expulsion of the Triumphant Beast*, 1584) he points out that it is change that produces pleasure and that pleasure lies in this crossing of opposites (*Giordano Bruno and the Philosophy of the Ass*, p.26 quoting from *Spaccio*)

"*every pleasure consists in nothing other than in a certain transition, passage, and movement. It is certain that the condition of hunger is painful and sad; unpleasant and heavy is the condition of satiety; yet pleasure is found in moving from one to the other. The state of ardent love torments, the state of fulfilled desire causes grief; but satisfaction comes in the transition from one state to the other*".

These words are echoed by Orsino (1.1.1-3)

> *If music be the food of love, play on,*
> *Give me excess of it, that surfeiting*
> *The appetite may sicken and so die*

and again (1.1.7-8)

> *Enough, no more,*
> *'Tis not so sweet now as it was before.*

Orsino is associated with transitions, with the changes in things (2.4.73-78) and he finds his match in Cesario who changes from Cesario to Viola, from male to female. Orsino seems a fickle character but it is love that makes him both inconstant and constant (2.4.17-20)

> *For such as I am all true lovers are,*
> *Unstaid and skittish in all motions else*
> *Save in the constant image of the creature*
> *That is beloved.*

He typifies the coincidence of opposites, he is changeable but his goal is constant. The constancy of his love allows him to navigate through changes and the uncertainty that comes from life.

What You Will

The alternate title for *Twelfth Night* is *What You Will*. This phrase can have several different meanings but there are two that are most easily associated with the play and its underlying philosophy. First, the phrase could imply the passive acceptance of a higher authority like God, Fate, Cupid, Duke or Countess and in fact all these apply at some point in the play as characters submit to the will of those with power over them (1.5.303-4)

> *Fate, show thy force, ourselves we do not owe,*
> *What is decreed must be*

and (2.2.40-41)

> *O time, thou must untangle this, not I.*

It is too hard a knot for me t'untie.

Or, secondly, the phrase could mean 'do what you will' i.e. 'do whatever pleases you'. You become the center of your universe; a type of anarchy where you are in charge and where what you choose to do defines who you are. This mantra with all its anarchic possibilities is Toby's *raison d'être* and why he is often seen as the lord of misrule. But it can equally apply to Feste or any of the other characters who are far more socially responsible in their decision making and in exercising their freedom to choose.

'What you will' also defines the two extremes of Bruno's philosophy; at one pole the passive acceptance of God's Will (negative asses) and at the other pole the individual's right to act and take control of their world (positive asses). The two extremes lie unspoken behind the narrative of the play but the choice of self-assertion (seen in both Viola and Olivia) or passive acceptance of a hierarchy (seen in Malvolio) is never far from the audience's mind.

Conclusion

Twelfth Night is a comic love story which at its heart is really an allegory about the search for truth, a truth that can lead to anarchy if abused or order if applied with empathy and love. The play dramatizes the fact that the core of any truth lies in our sense of self, since all the knowledge we have of the world comes to us through our senses; in essence all the world is filtered through our 'selves'. To be able to navigate in a world full of deception, such as the world presented to us in the play, we must know first who we are. Only from the certainty of knowing ourselves can we hope to know the world (5.1.145)

Be that thou knowst thou art.

Our selves or our souls are the only constant, the one knowable that is available to us. The play demonstrates this by showing us that appearances, actions and words can all be deceptive. We are adrift in a sea of uncertainty.

Bruno's philosophy of learned ignorance, that we are all asses or fools underlies Shakespeare's play. A play that is carefully constructed around a cast of fools; fools for love (Orsino, Olivia, Viola), professional fools (Feste), drunkard fools (Sir Toby), natural fools (Sir Andrew), and circumstantial fools (Malvolio). All Shakespeare's cast gets into difficulty because they lack knowledge, they do not have the information they need to make correct decisions (4.2.42-43)

no darkness / but ignorance.

They have all been deceived or deluded (intentionally or unintentionally) by those around them. The only way out of this situation lies in the acceptance of the fact that you are a fool, only then can you begin to learn what is going on. By accepting that you can never know precisely what is happening allows you to begin learning equipped with a healthy dose of skepticism. You can begin your journey to certainty by first understanding your inner self, your soul through which all the world is filtered. By knowing yourself you can begin to free yourself of delusions, of false perceptions, that colour your world view. It is the epiphanies at the end of *Twelfth Night* that finally allows the characters to see one another as their true selves; the false veils have been lifted, the schemes and their perpetrators have been exposed.

Bruno's philosophy that all souls are equal resonates through the play and justifies marriages that may be questionable in a strict hierarchy; both Olivia and Orsino marry below their degree but they both marry their equals in that they see their 'selves' reflected in the souls of their beloved, Sebastian and Viola, respectively. Bruno's belief in the equality of souls is reflected in the epiphany that Cesario is Viola, that a man can be a woman. This is reiterated in the story of the twins, that a male and female twin can be so alike as to be indistinguishable by the cast. Shakespeare's play depicts a world where the differences between men and women show themselves to be irrelevant at least in the makeup of their souls.

The happy ending Shakespeare supplies is only possible because the play is infused with Bruno's democratizing transmigrating soul of the Cellenican Ass. A soul that could be anyone at any time. In a story of deception the strict hierarchy that Malvolio both trusts in and hopes to violate can be seen as the greatest deception of all for Malvolio is shown the truth of our universal soul by Feste. It is a truth that threatens the hierarchy that Malvolio has grown to admire. If he continues to believe that one person is fundamentally better than another (as he believes he is better than everyone else) then he does in fact risk being seen as mad in a world that is quickly adapting to a new reality.

Bruno's Pythagorean based philosophies of learned ignorance and transmigrating souls although not explicitly mentioned do contribute a unity to Shakespeare's play. They add a level of understanding that smoothes out the wrinkles and rationalizes much of what happens in the play. The fact that Bruno, the man, as well as his published works were available in England and known by a wide circle of Shakespeare's associates (Sir Philip Sidney, Sir Fulke Greville, John Florio, etc.) does suggest Shakespeare would be familiar with his ideas; ideas that were highly controversial and the subject of much debate.

Bruno's poetic belief in the coincidence of contraries as a philosophical principal would surely attract the attention of any poet and the transitory nature of the idea would be hard to resist. *Twelfth Night* is rife with these contraries as the female Viola becomes the male Cesario, as Orsino's love for Olivia transforms into hate (5.1.113-127), as the austere Malvolio becomes the ridiculous. These circular conceits can also be seen in Shakespeare's use of language, *deadly life* (1.5.257), *proper false* (2.2.29), *beauteous evil* (3.4.366), and *fair cruelty* (1.5.280). These are not just oxymorons, their use in plot development tells us they are bred in the very bone of the play. Bearing all this in mind it is difficult to deny Shakespeare had a working knowledge of Bruno's philosophies.

Bruno tempered knowledge with ignorance - showing we could not know everything. Shakespeare wrote *Twelfth Night* as a 'slice of life' where not all the questions were answered. We, as an audience, are satisfied by the love story but we never find out what happens to Antonio, Malvolio, or Andrew Aguecheek. We are left to project; our knowledge is tempered with ignorance.

For Bruno the symbol of divine revelation, of epiphany, was the Ass; for Shakespeare *Twelfth Night* was a story profuse with epiphanies, its very title designed to allude to the Day of Epiphany and whose characters are all asses. The connection between the two, their shared sense of the soul, their shared understanding of an uncertainty that pervades the created world, their love of coincident opposites, all seem too close to deny that Bruno did not have an influence on the thoughts and ideas found in Shakespeare's Twelfth Night.

Footnotes

[1] Bruno reiterates Nicholas of Cusa in *The Cabala of Pegasus*, First Dialogue, p. 52

"the ultimate knowledge is the assured assessment that one cannot know anything and does not know anything, consequently to recognize that one can be nothing but an ass and is nothing but an ass; to which end came the Socratics".

Bibliography

1) *Twelfth Night or What You Will,* edited by Keir Elam, The Arden Shakespeare, third edition, Cengage Learning , 2008.
2) *Twelfth Night, New Critical Essays*, edited by James Schiffer, Shakespeare Criticism Vol. 34, Routledge, 2011.
   Included in this work are essays of specific interest:
   Introduction: Taking the long view: 'Twelfth Night' criticism and performance by James Schiffer.
   'Twelfth Night': editing puzzles and eunuchs of all kinds by Patricia Parker.
   "His fancy's queen" sensing sexual strangeness in 'Twelfth Night' by Bruce R. Smith.
   Madness and social mobility in 'Twelfth Night' by Ivo Kamps.
   Whodunit? Plot, plotting and detection in 'Twelfth Night' by Cynthia Lewis.
3) *The Elizabethan World Picture,* E.M.W.Tillyard, Chapt. 5, Vintage Books, 1964.
4) *Imagination in the English Renaissance: Psychology and Poetic*, William Rossky, *Studies in the Renaissance*, Vol. 5, 1958, p. 49-73.
5) *Commentary on Plato's Symposium on Love*, Marsilio Ficino, translated by Sears Jayne, Spring Publications Inc., 1985.
6) *Giordano Bruno and the Philosophy of the Ass*, Nuccio Ordine, translated by Henryk Baranski and Arielle Saiber, Yale University Press, New Haven and London, 1996.
7) *The Cabala of Pegasus*, Giordano Bruno, translated and annotated by Sidney L. Sondergard and Madison U. Sowell, Yale University Press, New Haven and London, 2002.

8) *Giordano Bruno and the Logic of Coincidence; Unity and Multiplicity in the Philosophical Thought of Giordano Bruno*, Antonio Calcagno, Peter Lang Publishing, 1998.

9) *Nicholas of Cusa on Learned Ignorance: A Translation and an Appraisal of De Docta Ignorantia*, Jasper Hopkins, The Arthur J. Banning Press, Minneapolis, 2nd edition, 1996.

10) *Plotinus: Complete Works*, Plotinus, translated Kenneth Sylvan Guthrie, London: George Bell and Sons, 1918.

11) *Shakespeare and Parmenides: The Metaphysics of Twelfth Night*, Walter N. King, *Studies in English Literature, 1500-1900*, Vol. 8, No. 2, Elizabethan and Jacobean Drama (Spring, 1968), p. 283-306.

12) *Psychology and the Human Dilemma*, Rollo May, Princeton, N.J., D. Van Nostrand, 1967.

The Comedy of Errors: Cross Purposes

Introduction

The Comedy of Errors is on its surface a classical work drawn from classical sources. It is a comical Roman farce rooted in the mistaken identities of two sets of twins. The play is often dismissed as a frivolous work full of physical slapstick and low comedy. Because of the play's complex structure many believe that its plot has superseded its content with the characters being used essentially to narrate this structure. Without dismissing these criticisms I will show that Shakespeare, when he set the play in Ephesus, added a layer of Christian content to the play's substructure that informed the play's overall content. By doing so he created a comedy that also offered insight into the human condition, lessons he learned from the morality play tradition. The 'Christian branding' brought with it the hope and optimism necessary for the comedy to work and softened some of the hard edges of its Roman origins. Shakespeare's use of Christian allusion adds meat to this farce's bones.

The Dark Frame

Shakespeare's play *The Comedy of Errors* takes advantage of a framing technique, a story that precedes the main storyline and then later contributes to its resolution. It houses the comedy within an enclosing darker narrative. This narrative creates some of the tension necessary for the comedy to effectively function; it adds the real world possibility that serious consequences may result even from the play's more comic antics. The frame also provides the backstory to the comedy so that this portion of the play can begin immediately without having to slow its pace with necessary exposition.

The frame sets up the play. All the concerns expressed in the frame will be elaborated on in the body of the play. The framing device is thematically integrated into the play and guides the play. To understand the spirit of the play it is necessary to carefully look at the ideas expressed in this framing device.

The frame tells the story of Egeon, a crosser, a man who crosses boundaries, in this case from Syracuse (his home) to Ephesus where he is detained and brought before the court. While elucidating his woes before the Duke he reveals the backstory of his twin sons and wife. The frame story begins by dropping us in the middle of a trade dispute between Syracuse and Ephesus. We are given no details of the dispute and are only told that any merchant originating from the other city state will have their goods seized and themselves executed if they cannot (through goods and coin) raise sufficient sum to ransom themselves to freedom. Two key concepts are presented here: the idea that money can buy freedom (life itself) and that people can arbitrarily be divided into two groups (us and the enemy) by a simple proclamation of law (1.1.13-22)

> *It hath in solemn synods been decreed,*
> *Both by the Syracusians and ourselves*
> *To admit no traffic to our adverse towns;*
> *Nay more, if any born at Ephesus*
> *Be seen at Syracusian marts and fairs;*
> *Again if any Syracusian born*
> *Come to the bay of Ephesus, he dies,*
> *His goods confiscate to the Duke's dispose,*
> *Unless a thousand marks be levied*
> *To quit the penalty and to ransom him.*

Within this frame these ideas are reiterated. Egeon tells of how he purchased two newborns (both named Dromio) to act as slaves for his own two sons (who both come to receive the name Antipholus); the division between free and slave being arbitrary for all the children were born free in Epidamnum and yet only Egeon's remained so (1.1.54-57)

A mean woman was delivered
Of such a burden male, twins both alike;
Those, for their parents were exceeding poor,
I bought, and brought up to attend my sons.

Egeon is therefore no stranger to the concept that a commercial transaction can purchase life. Just as the synods arbitrarily made Egeon an enemy of Ephesus, Egeon arbitrarily made the two Dromios slaves to the two Antipholi twins and equally arbitrarily did Nature separate Egeon from his wife and one of his sons (1.1.78-79; 81-85; 101-106)

My wife more careful for the latter-born,
Had fasten'd him unto a small spare mast...
To him one of the other twins was bound,
Whilst I had been like heedful of the other.
The children thus dispos'd, my wife and I,
Fixing our eyes on whom our care was fix'd,
Fasten'd ourselves at either end the mast...
We were encounter'd by a mighty rock,
Which being violently borne upon,
Our helpful ship was splitted in the midst;
So that in this unjust divorce of us,
Fortune had left to both of us alike
What to delight in, what to sorrow for.

Egeon refers to this divorce as 'unjust', a word that percolates through all three arbitrary separations, suggesting that both humans and the gods are unjust.

Shakespeare's frame has spelled out the arbitrary nature of how individuals can be assigned the label of citizen and enemy, granted freedom or slavery, and fated to life or death.

When Egeon finishes his story he sums it up by saying (1.1.118)

Thus have you heard me sever'd from my bliss.

His bliss lies with his family: wife and children. He doesn't mention his loss of fortune. Egeon's shipwreck has clarified his priorities but not ended his trials. He then updates us and tells of when his '*youngest boy*' reached '*eighteen years*' and of how he became '*inquisitive after his brother*' and went '*in quest of him*'. Egeon tells us once again of how he was separated from the one '*whom he loved* ' for the hope of hearing news of the other twin who he would '*love to see*' (1.1.130-131).

From the text it appears that Egeon's son is gone seven years (5.1.320) but that after waiting two years Egeon begins his own search for one or both of his sons (1.1.132-136)

Five summers have I spent in farthest Greece,
Roaming clean through the bounds of Asia,
And coasting homeward came to Ephesus
Hopeless to find, yet loth to leave unsought
Or that or any place that harbours men.

This part of the tale is a revelation to the Duke. It tells him of how Egeon has come to Ephesus; he is not a commercial trader but a father in search of a lost son. Egeon's journey reveals something more to us, it shows us how Shakespeare has linked Egeon's trip to that of St. Paul's, a.k.a. Saul who literally 'saw the light' on the road to Damascus. Saint Paul travelled widely through Greece and Asia also arriving at Ephesus (Acts 18:1, 18 and Acts 19:1-2)

After these things Paul departed from Athens, and came to Corinth...and then took his leave of the brethren, and sailed thence into Syria...Paul having passed through the upper coasts came to Ephesus: and finding certain disciples, He said unto them, Have ye received the Holy Ghost since ye believed?

The frame has included this very powerful allusion. It is both an allusion to *The Epistle of Paul to The Ephesians* and an allusion to baptism by the Holy Ghost into the Spirit of God. Ideas contained in *Ephesians* and thoughts concerning the Pentecost will be revisited in the body of the play. Patricia Parker (*Shakespeare from the Margins*) also notes that the entire play takes place in what she calls the 'space of doom'. By this she is referring to the one day the Duke has granted Egeon to find someone to ransom him (redeem him) before his execution. She sees this doom as an allusion to tales of the Apocalypse, the end of the world marked by the Second Coming.

So Shakespeare's frame story has provided us with an index to his primary images and has hinted at the Christian armature from which he will hang Plautus' plots. The play is full of biblical allusions. These do not just function as clever word play added to amuse a Christian audience but they are structural in that they place a biblical space of waiting for redemption from Doom onto the essentially comic Roman farce.

Plautus' Plot

The Arden Shakespeare (*The Comedy of Errors*, edited by R.A. Foakes, Introduction, III. The Sources, p.xxiv-xxxiv, 2007) discusses the source material for *The Comedy of Errors* citing Plautus' *Menaechmi* and his *Amphitruo* for their plot structures. Arden supplies summaries of the action of these two plays in its Appendix (ibid, p. 109-115). Arden also points out that the story of Apollonius of Tyre found in John Gower's *Confessio Amantis* (1554) may have provided the plot details for the framing story of Egeon and Emilia (ibid, p. xxxi).

Although plot drives a play and this particular play is to a large extent plot driven it does not reveal to the audience why the play was written. The plot supports but does not explain the purpose of a play. The purpose of a play is usually more than just to entertain; it often informs, it allows the audience to rehearse possible futures and allows them to see the world through another's eyes. When a playwright changes the setting of his source material, in this case from Epidamnum to Ephesus, it is done for specific reasons (otherwise why bother). In this instance it suggests he wants his audience to recall *The New Testament* book of *Ephesians*.

The Arden Edition includes relevant passages from *The New Testament* concerning Ephesus that Shakespeare took advantage of when constructing his play. Arden views it as source material but of course it is more than just that; it offers us a key to unlocking this play's particular purpose.

Biblical Allusions in a Time of Waiting

In her book, *Shakespeare from the Margins,* Parker elaborates on the biblical allusions that fill the pages of *The Comedy of Errors*. They spill out of the dark frame and into the main text. These biblical allusions add a seriousness to the frivolity of the Roman farce. The farce is the human condition, the condition of not knowing. Shakespeare chose to make this farce the backdrop on which he added a biblical narrative. To understand this purpose it is first necessary to examine some of the allusions employed.

These allusions are specific in that they refer to the specific place, Ephesus, and a specific time, the end of the world/ second coming, as well they refer to specific types of relationships such as that between a husband and wife or between twin brothers. The allusions are intentional, numerous, and focused. They constitute the spiritual part of the play. The materialistic side of the play will be examined later along with a discussion on how this dualism (one of many) finds resolution in a type of unity.

The biblical allusions are so numerous that they are probably best dealt with in a sequential manner, in the order they appear as the play unfolds. *The Comedy of Errors* begins with a double error. The error results when Dromio-Ephesus is confused with Dromio-Syracuse by his master Antipholus-Syracuse, and Antipholus-S. is in turn mistaken by Dromio-E. for his master, Antipholus-Ephesus. This crossing of identities leads to arguing at cross purposes as Antipholus-S. questions Dromio-E. as to where he took his money while Dromio-E. tries to get Antipholus-S. to come home to a dinner he is late for. Dromio-E. announces that his master's household has been fasting and praying for his return (1.2.89-90)

She that doth fast till you come home to dinner,
And prays that you will hie you home to dinner.

This first error leads to the first biblical allusion: it is an unmistakable reference to the period known as the biblical interim, a time of patient waiting, fasting and praying by the church in anticipation of Christ's return. This return is also figured in the exchange between Luciana and Adriana, the sister-in-law and wife of Antipholus-E., respectively (2.1.43-44)

Luc.: *Here comes your man, now is your husband nigh.*
(Enter Dromio-E.)
Adr.: *Say, is your tardy master now at hand?*

At the Apocalyptic Doom, the World's End, the end of time, the master (Christ) returns for his bride (the church).

So what Patricia Parker has suggested is that it is in the 'space of doom' created in the framing device (Egeon's one day before his execution) that the rest of the play occurs and that this play therefore mimics humanities wait for Christ's return and Judgment Day. One can sense this in the main text because it is full of waiting, delays, and confusion; characters wander through the city just as all of humanity wanders through life (1.2.30-31)

I will go lose myself,

And wander up and down to view the city.

Most importantly however is that Christian ideas of the interim (waiting for Christ's return) have become integrated with the Plautine farce through several verbal linkages (*I Corinthians* 16:8)

But I will tarry at Ephesus until Pentecost.

Scene by scene Parker points out the parallels that exist between biblical sources and *The Comedy of Errors*. The accumulation of these echoes points to a clear direction and theme in Shakespeare's work. It is the focus and repetition of these images that indicate a purpose to the work. By examining some of these linkages between the play and its biblical allusions a pattern emerges.

In Act (1.2) here we find a devout Mistress fasting, praying and watching for the return of her Master. This alludes to the many stories of waiting for the return of Christ such as the one in (*Mark* 13:33-37)

33 Take ye heed, watch and pray: for ye know not when the time is.

34 For the Son of man is as a man taking a far journey, who left his house, and gave authority to his servants, and to every man his work, and commanded the porter to watch.

35 Watch ye therefore: for ye know not when the master of the house cometh, at even, or at midnight, or at the cockcrowing, or in the morning:

36 Lest coming suddenly he find you sleeping.

37 And what I say unto you I say unto all, Watch.

In Act (2.1) we overhear a discussion between Luciana and Adriana concerning the role of a wife. In it Luciana alludes to St. Paul's advice regarding spouses' duty towards one another as stated in (*Ephesians* 5:21-29)

21 Submitting yourselves one to another in the fear of God.

22 Wives, submit yourselves unto your own husbands, as unto the Lord.

23 For the husband is the head of the wife, even as Christ is the head of the church: and he is saviour of the body.

24 Therefore as the church is subject unto Christ, so let the wives be to their own husbands in everything.

25 Husband, love your wives, even as Christ also loved the church, and gave himself for it;

26 That he might sanctify and cleanse it with the washing of water by the word,

27 That he might present it to himself a glorious church, not having spot, or winkle, or any such thing; but that it should be holy and without blemish.

28 So ought men to love their wives as their own bodies. He that loveth his wife loveth himself.

The advice in *Ephesians* is balanced; wives love your husbands like Christ – husbands love your wives as Christ loved the Church; as you would, in fact, love yourself. Mutual sacrifice for each other and mutual support.

The audience would recall these passages from *Ephesians* the moment Luciana and Adriana began their discussion about marriage. They would have recognized the imbalance in Adriana's and Antipholus' marriage. Roles are understandably different but balance and mutual respect was essential.

When Adriana employs her water metaphor (2.2.125-129)

For know, my love, as easy mayst thou fall
A drop of water in the breading gulf,
And take unmingled thence that drop again
Without addition or diminishing,

> *As take from me thyself, and not me too*

she is evoking the idea that they are one flesh, indivisible and echoing the water imagery in verses 26, 27 above. This idea of intermingling and staining is further explored in (2.2.142-144)

> *For if we two be one, and thou play false,*
> *I do digest the poison of thy flesh,*
> *Being strumpeted by thy contagion.*

Whatever sin Antipholus commits stains them both. Shakespeare conflates the ideas of one flesh with the unity and cleanliness of water while at the same time echoing the biblical passages above with the commonplace of (*Mark* 10:8)

> *And they twain shall be one flesh: so then they are no more twain, but one flesh.*

Act (2.2) concerns a discussion about time, there being a time for everything, echoing (*Ecclesiastes* 3:1-8)

> *To everything there is a season...*

This scene involves extensive punning between 'hair' and 'heir' and makes allusion to the twins Jacob and Esau and how 'smooth' Jacob fooled their father Isaac by disguising himself in another's hair to appear like the elder twin 'hairy' Esau to claim his blessing. The story reveals how a hairy man was outwitted by a usurping brother and how he lost his right as elder son or heir. This explains much of the wordplay concerning wit and hair (2.2.81-82)

> *Why, but there's many a man hath more hair*
> *than wit.*

Act (2.2) also reveals how a couple even though 'one flesh' can still be deceived about identity. The false Antipholus-S. is mistaken by Adriana for her husband Antipholus-E. and is admitted into their house. This scene has parallels with the biblical warning to those who cannot distinguish between the real and false Christs that will come in the interim (*Matthew* 24:5-6)

For many shall come in my name, saying, I am Christ; and shall deceive many...

but the end is not yet.

The scene also makes a direct reference to *"the world's end"* (2.2.106)

In Act (3.1) we find Antipholus-E. barred from his own house because his doppelganger was previously welcomed in as a result of the aforementioned misidentification. The scene becomes the comic opposite of (*Matthew* 7:7)

Knock and it shall be opened unto you.

Throughout this scene there is repeated reference made to the patience that is required of us. This is a constant refrain both in *The Comedy of Errors* and in the biblical sources when referring to this time of waiting (*Revelation* 2:2,3)

I know thy works, and thy labour, and thy patience...

...and hast patience, and for my name's sake hast laboured, and hast not fainted.

For Antipholus-E. this period of waiting is also a period of exclusion where a wall physically separates him from his family. What is a physical wall in Shakespeare's play is a metaphorical wall in *Ephesians* (*Ephesians* 2:11,12,14-16,19).

11 Wherefore remember, that ye being in time past Gentiles...

12 That at that time ye were without Christ, being aliens from the commonwealth of Israel, and strangers from the covenants of promise, having no hope, and without God in the world:

14 For he is our peace, who hath made both one, and hath broken down the middle wall of partition between us;

15 Having abolished in his flesh the enmity, even the law of commandments contained in ordinances; for to make in himself of twain one new man, so making peace;

16 And that he might reconcile both unto God in one body by the cross...

19 Now therefore ye are no more strangers and foreigners, but fellow citizens...of the household of God.

The argument made in *Ephesians* is that Christ through his sacrifice unites the disparate groups and overthrows the authoritarian law of the Old Testament.

Parker also believes this 'wall of partition' story to be tied in to the Biblical story of Jacob and Esau, the twin brothers of *Genesis*. It is a story of younger and elder twins that become separated from one another. Esau and his descendents became the Edomites (*Genesis* 36:1-43) and Jacob, who changed his name to Israel, became the father of the Israelites (*Genesis* 35:10-11).

This division of one family into Gentile and Jew is mimicked in *The Comedy of Errors*. Twins born in Epidamnum become Ephesian and Syracusian, legislated enemies whose presence on the others' soil means death. Parker believes this Jewish/Gentile divide can be linked to *Ephesians* where we are told of their subsequent reunification.

The image of the 'closed doors' also recalls the parable of the foolish virgins (*Matthew* 25:1-13) who return too late to the wedding, after the bridegroom has come, and find the door shut against them. They knock but the bridegroom answers

"I know you not".

In our story it is Adriana who shoos an unseen Antipholus-E. away (3.1.64)

Your wife, sir knave? go, get you from the door.

Later in Act (3.2) we find Luciana trying to council Antipholus-S. (who she believes to be Antipholus-E.) to engage in deception in order to secure her sister's (Adriana's) happiness. In a general way it mimics the temptation of Christ (*Matthew* 4:1-11) in that innocence is threatened by gile (3.2.36-37)

> *The folded meaning of your words' deceit.*
> *Against my soul's pure truth, why labour you...*

Many of these allusions draw from the same well; they pertain to Christ's return, the end of days, and the coming new order. The Apocalypse occurs when Christ (the husband) returns for his bride (the church). In the previously quoted *Ephesians* 5:21-29 it was again Christ and the church that stood in for husband and wife. The church at Ephesus also rates highly in *Revelation* where it gets a shout out by Christ speaking through St. John praising its patience and offering advice (*Revelation* 2:1-7).

There is a strong referential relationship between both *Ephesians* and *Revelation* and *The Comedy of Errors*. In Act 3.2 we find a description of Nell that has many equivalents in the *Book of Revelation*. Many of her qualifiers match those of the whore of Babylon (*Revelations* 17) *"she being a very beastly creature"* (3.2.85-86) unclean and *"o'er-embellished with rubies, carbuncles, sapphires"* (3.2.131-132) and most importantly *"if she lives till doomsday she'll burn a week longer than the whole world"* (3.2.97-98). The description is comic but the reference is clear.

Dromio in this same dialogue makes a further association by alluding to the vigilance we all must show in the time before the second coming. It is spoken of in (*Ephesians* 6:13-17)

> *Wherefore take unto you the whole armour of God...having your loins girt about with truth, and having on the breastplate of righteousness...shield of faith...helmet of salvation.*

Dromio echoes this in the line (3.2.144-146)

I think, if my breast had not been made of faith, and my heart of steel...

These linkages rely on word association and shared imagery. It is a connection that is designed to sit at the back of your mind as you watch/read the play. In a time when everyone knew their Bible these images would be easily recognizable and part of a shared consciousness. They were meant to operate at the periphery like background music. They created a mood that sat just below the surface of the play's comic antics and hinted at its overall theme.

Act 4 is concerned mainly with the gold chain. This chain becomes a symbol associated with acts that delay or detain the various characters in the play. The chain is a diversion that introduces concerns about the material world. The chain also binds characters together through love, indebtedness and the law. The chain's role as an unpaid debt ties this main text back to the framing story of Egeon and his unpaid debt.

The language involved in this act is biblical in nature relating to sin, deliverance, and punishment. Dromio is sent for *"angels"* or gold coins to *"deliver"* Antipholus-E. from arrest (4.3.38-39) where he is kept *"in Tartar limbo"* (4.2.32) by *"one that, before the judgment, carries poor souls to hell"* (4.2.40).

Later in Dromio's discussion about time with Adriana we are given another reference to the judgment day (*Revelation* 3:3)

If therefore thou shalt not watch, I will come on thee as a thief, and thou shalt not know what hour I will come upon thee

but here time is presented as the thief (4.2.59-60)

Nay, he's a thief too; have you not heard men say
That time comes stealing on by night and day?

These biblical allusions continue to pile up in the next scene. The main ones of interest are, firstly, that of the prodigal son (*Luke* 15:11-32) which tells a tale of a wandering son, his brother, their father and of their subsequent reunion. The second allusion from this same scene refers to the story of Adam, after the fall, living in skins, suffering in the prison of the world, and under the Law of the Old Testament before Christ and redemption (4.3.16-18)

> *Not that Adam that kept the paradise, but that*
> *Adam that keeps the prison; he that goes in the*
> *calf's-skin that was killed for the prodigal.*

This second allusion to the 'offending Adam' is also a reference to 'the old man' of *Ephesians* a reference which hints at the theme of transformation (*Ephesians* 4:22,24)

> *That ye put off concerning the former conversation the old man which is corrupt according to the deceitful lusts;*
>
> *And that ye put on the new man, which after God is created in righteousness and true holiness.*

More biblical echoes occur as Dromio-S. and Antipholus-S. attempt to flee the city. First they encounter the Courtesan, symbol of the Great Whore of Revelation. They charge her with being Satan (4.3.46) and of appearing like an angel but only to deceive them (4.3.53-55). This references (*2Corinthians* 11:13-14)

> *For such are false apostles, deceitful workers, transforming themselves into the apostles of Christ.*
>
> *And no marvel; for Satan himself is transformed into an angel of light.*

This quotation regarding mistaken and transformed identities is in keeping with the storyline and adds to the chaotic mood of uncertainty. The characters, at this point, are uncertain about what is happening and why people are treating them in such unpredictable ways. Of course the comedy of the play depends on this exact type of dislocation; each character is speaking into a context that is at odds with their expectations.

It is out of this confusion that accusations of sorcery and witchcraft are leveled by Antipholus-S. and Dromio-S. against the Courtesan. They, in turn, appear completely mad to her (4.3.78)

> *Now out of doubt that Antipholus is mad.*

This madness makes Antipholus subject to accusation of demon possession and leads to scenes of his exorcism (4.4.52-53)

> *I charge thee Satan, hous'd within this man,*
> *To yield possession to my holy prayers*

which in turn echoes *Acts* 19:11-17 which tells of St. Paul's holy works in Ephesus and of the false exorcists that practiced in his name.

Act 5 brings the play to its conclusion. It is at this point that the frame story and the comedy of errors converge literally at the place of doom, where Egeon is to be executed. The allusions to the end of the world and the second coming find their fulfillment here.

Emilia speaks of the intervening years as a time of travail (5.1.400-402)

> *Thirty-three years have I gone in travail*
> *Of you, my sons, and tell this present hour*
> *My heavy burden ne'er delivered.*

Thirty-three years is the span of Christ's life on earth, the time of his travail and wandering. Now is the time the twins meet. This is when the wall of partition comes down. This is the epiphany that comes with the end of times (*1Corinthians* 13:10, 12)

> *But when that which is perfect is come, then that which is in part shall be done away.*

> *For now we see through a glass, darkly; but then face to face: now I know in part; but then shall I know even as also I am known.*

The second coming is equated with perfect knowledge and unity. The accusations of demon possession and witchcraft all fall away. All the conflict in the play is seen for what it is: errors resulting from mistaken identity.

The second coming is really the coming of the twins' second selves. It is a revelation that leads to the reunification of the family.

Before examining the last scene of *The Comedy of Errors* it is important to look once again at the very first error of the play; it is a double error, one about a tardy master (alluding to the spiritual side of the play) and the other about the whereabouts of money (alluding to the material side of the play). It is this material world we must now examine so that we can properly understand how these two worlds intersect in the final act. The material world will reveal much about equity and transformation necessary in informing the conclusion.

Inequality

The world of *The Comedy of Errors* is one that is fundamentally inequitable. It is a merchant's world where everything is monetized, from the life of a prisoner to the affections of a courtesan. It is a world where money is power and power is liberty. It is a world where females lack the same liberty as permitted their male counterparts (2.1.10) and where even monarchs are subject to synods (like parliament) (1.1.97).

Eric Heinze perceives *The Comedy of Errors* to be structured on various dualisms such as master-servant, husband-wife, native-alien, parent-child, buyer-seller, and monarch-parliament. Each dualism represents a type of power structure that is established by social norms and backed by force of law. Power and liberty being distributed according to the wealth it represents.

The war between Ephesus and Syracuse appears to be a trade war and money features in most of the disputes that arise in the play. Wealth factors into most of the relationships, it is used to elicit affection (3.2.5-6)

> *If you did wed my sister for her wealth,*
> *Then for her wealth's sake use her with more kindness.*

It is used to punish (3.1.117-119)

> *...that chain will I bestow*
> *(Be it for nothing but to spite my wife)*
> *Upon mine hostess there.*

It is used to compliment and seduce (3.2.48)

> *Spread o'er the silver waves thy golden hairs.*

It is used to create suspense and tension in the play (1.2.105)

> *I greatly fear my money is not safe.*

It, one thousand marks, can buy a life (1.1.23-24; 153-154)

> *Thy substance, valued at the highest rate,*
> *Cannot amount unto a hundred marks;*
> *Beg thou, or borrow, to make up the sum,*
> *And live; if no, then thou art doom'd to die.*

Gold fuels the action just as mistaken identity drives the plot. Gold gets people arrested and is capable of getting them released; it is also one of the subjects of the very first 'error' in the comedy.

The error, which is twofold, results when Dromio-E. is confused with Dromio-S. by his master Antipholus-S. Antipholus-S. is worried about his money while Dromio-E. just wishes to hurry his master home. This very first 'error' splits the play into spiritual and material concerns which manifest themselves through the play's language and allusions. As Dromio-E. tries to get his tardy master home to dinner, Antipholus-S. can only focus on his money which he is increasingly concerned over

> (1.2.54) *Where have you left the money that I gave you?*
> (1.2.59) *Tell me, and dally not, where is the money?*
> (1.2.70) *Where is the gold I gave in charge to thee?*

(1.2.105) *I greatly fear my money is not safe.*

This first 'error' of the play is not just the confusion of identities but it represents a confusion of responsibilities - domestic versus commercial. As a general rule it appears that Antipholus-E. prioritizes business over his family relationships and the material over the spiritual. This behaviour stands in contrast with that of Antipholus-S. who has chosen to engage in a perilous search for his lost family over any of his personal concerns; he has in essence put his own identity (career, wife, family) on hold while he searches for a lost brother and mother (1.2.39-40)

So I, to find a mother and a brother,
In quest of them, unhappy, lose myself.

Antipholus-S. has deferred his own life for family while Antipholus-E. has turned his back on his own family. The crossing over of identities brings these hidden tensions to light.

Dromio-E. relates a comic version of his discussion with Antipholus to Adriana but it ends in a sad truth unknowingly revealed by the wrong Antipholus (2.1.67-68; 71)

"My mistress, sir...", quoth I; "hang up thy mistress;
I know not thy mistress, out on thy mistress..."
"I know", quoth he, "no house, no wife, no mistress".

What is said truthfully by one Antipholus reveals a secret belief held by the other Antipholus. The crossing of identities leads to a revelation that feels like the truth to Adriana who has felt neglected by her work-obsessed husband. She, unfortunately, sees herself like a fungible commodity that can be wasted if not used (2.1.90). She feels she is only as desirable as the clothing he provides her with. She is the armature from which wealth hangs and is only as beautiful as the wealth she represents (2.1.94-95)

Do their gay vestments his affections bait?

That's not my fault, he's master of my state.

She fears she is only as valued as she is valuable.

This fear is not unfounded, in a discussion between Antipholus-E. and Balthazar he reveals his materialistic concerns. For where Balthazar values company (3.1.21, 23)

> *I hold your dainties cheap, sir, and your welcome dear*
> *Good meat, sir, is common; that every churl affords.*

Antipholus values the material (3.1.24-25)

> *And welcome more common, for that's nothing*
> *but words.*

In this world where everything is seen as a commodity Antipholus-S. also sees time as such, essentially remarking that 'time is money', when he chastises Dromio-S. for wasting his (2.2.28-29)

> *Your sauciness will jest upon my love,*
> *And make common of my serious hours.*

To paraphrase he means 'How dare you take advantage of my kindness and treat my hours of business as common property which you waste with your high jinks'. This scene then carries on to a discussion about time *"There's a / time for all things"* (2.2.63-64) a statement Dromio-S. does not agree with for he points out that (2.2.71-72)

> *There's no time for a man to recover his hair*
> *that grows bald by nature.*

This joke hints at a more serious truth concerning a lost 'heir' and the time that could have been spent with them. Dromio is pointing out that time is not like a commodity; once time has passed it is gone forever. Antipholus-S. will never recover the time he could have spent growing up with Antipholus-E. nor will E. ever recover time he could have spent with Adriana. It is both a joke and a warning. It also acts as a point of departure for a series of biblical allusions that were examined earlier.

Money, power and privilege define each character in *The Comedy of Errors* and each is described accordingly (see Heinze, *Legal Studies*, Vol. 29). The patriarchal males are given reign over the entire globe (2.1.20-21)

Man, more divine, the master of all these,
Lord of the wide world and wild wat'ry seas.

This globe shrinks considerably when the characters are servants. Dromio's globe shrinks to the size of a football field and his world consists of nothing but running back and forth between masters that beat him (2.1.81-84)

Am I so round with you, as you with me,
That like a football you do spurn me thus?
You spurn me hence, and he will spurn me hither;
If I last in this service you must case me in leather.

As we go down the social ladder we see that Nell's world, a kitchen wench, is even smaller than Dromio's football field. Her world is defined by her own body (3.2.112-113)

she is spherical, like a globe; I could find out
countries in her.

The humour is low but all these stories are connected through the diminishing globe imagery, an imagery which ties into the play's framing device. In the frame, Egeon, a prisoner, finds his life pared down to a single day, one turning of the globe (1.1.150; 153-154)

I'll limit thee this day
...to make up the sum,
And live, if no, then thou art doom'd to die.

Power enjoys both scope and privilege while the under classes become the most visibly abused group in the play specifically the Dromios. The Dromios are unjustly punished and disrespected throughout the play and although the play does not directly address master responsibilities it is clear that Shakespeare wanted a subtext that did.

Shakespeare chose to set his play in Ephesus rather than Epidamnum where Plautus set the original play. Shakespeare also purposefully drew content and imagery out of the biblical *Ephesians* so that his audience would recall these scriptures and keep them at the back of their minds while they watched the play.

The advice given to masters and slaves is pointed and balance is demanded (*Ephesians* 6:5-9)

5 Servants, be obedient to them that are your masters according to the flesh, with fear and trembling, in singleness of your heart, as unto Christ;

6 Not with eyeservice, as menpleasers; but as the servant of Christ doing the will of God from the heart;

7 With good will doing service, as to the Lord, and not to men:

8 Knowing that whatsoever good thing any man doeth, the same shall he receive of the Lord, whether he be bond or free.

9 And, ye masters, do the same things unto them, forebearing threatening: knowing that your Master also is in heaven; neither is there respect of persons with him.

The balance is clear – do good service unto each other – with the Lord keeping count and not caring as to who is bond or free.

The themes of marriage, treatment of slaves and reunification are all addressed in Plautus but with the inclusion of biblical sources they are then stacked one atop the other. *The Comedy of Errors* both informs and broadens the content of the secular material by adding a dimension of spiritual responsibility into the mix. The inclusion hints at a future judgment day and a warning of the need to be equitable.

Equity

Although much of what we see in Ephesus is inequitable there are hints of balance. Adriana accuses Luciana of remaining single (avoiding the servitude of marriage) in order to keep her liberty (2.1.26)

This servitude makes you to keep unwed.

This accusation suggests that single women did enjoy more freedom than their married counterparts.

Antipholus-E. appears to take Adriana for granted and is contemptuous of both her schedule and decisions yet others like Balthazar hold her in high esteem respecting her history of wise judgments. He councils Antipholus to grant her the benefit of the doubt on any action she has taken (3.1.89-93)

...your long experience of her wisdom,
Her sober virtue, years and modesty,
Plead on her part some cause to you unknown;
And doubt not, sir, but she will well excuse
Why at this time the doors are made against you.

Balthazar respects Adriana and with that respect comes balance. He believes she has locked the doors against her husband for some (yet unknown) good reason.

Another example of equity is in the application of commercial law. A foreigner, referred to only as Second Merchant, bound for Persia has an officer of Ephesus arrest Angelo, a citizen, for non-payment of a debt. In regards to the law foreigners are equal to citizens (4.1.69-70)

Mer.: *Well, officer, arrest him at my suit*
Off.: *I do.*

Equity is also hinted at through the actions of the women in the play. Although the women are presented as subservient to the men their actions reveal something else; it is Nell who claims Dromio and puts him on the run (3.2.79-81)

> *I am due to a*
> *woman, one that claims me, one that haunts me, one*
> *that will have me*

it is Adriana who has Antipholus-E. bound (4.4.105)

> *O bind him, bind him, let him not come near me*

and it is Emilia that grants sanctuary to the men (5.1.94-96)

> *He took this place for sanctuary,*
> *And it shall privilege him from your hands*
> *Till I have brought him to his wits again.*

This subtle presence of equity/balance is unremarkable and it never emotionally engages us as much as the injustices do but they are enough to make the injustices stand out as unreasonable and unbalanced. This is why the repeated references to *The New Testament* epistle to the *Ephesians* is so important to understanding the play. It provides us with a baseline or model of what is appropriate behaviour.

Repeated statements are made in *Ephesians* that God does not discriminate between bonded and free persons but sees them as 'fellow citizens in the household of God'. All this subtext is in place so that Shakespeare could take on his next big theme, that of transformation, and by so doing suggest how a flawed society can change and find reunification.

Transformation

Ephesus is a place associated with magic. This connection comes by way of *The New Testament* (*Acts* 19: 13,19,28). Ephesus is a place of exorcists, practitioners of the curious arts, and home to the Temple of Diana and her followers. Shakespeare exaggerates this in the mind of Antipholus-S. to increase his unease in this foreign port (1.2.97-102)

> *They say this town is full of cozenage,*
> *As nimble jugglers that deceive the eye,*

> *Dark-working sorcerers that change the mind,*
> *Soul-killing witches that deform the body,*
> *Disguised cheaters, prating mountebanks,*
> *And many such-like liberties of sin.*

These preconceived ideas make him suspicious of anyone he comes into contact with; he is on guard and cautious with those he meets. This prejudice makes Antipholus-S. fear, perhaps more than normal, for his money and the law against Syracusians makes him fear for his life. He is a man on edge and justifiably paranoid. Although he has been searching for his brother for seven years he now starts to feel the impossibility of the task (1.2.35-38) so it is conceivable that he is also feeling a little despair. All these concerns create a heavy emotional load for Antipholus-S. and place him under enormous stress.

According to Robert O'Brien, Antipholus-S. begins to doubt his sense of reality not long after his arrival in port. In Ephesus he finds it increasingly difficult to interpret what people are saying to him (2.2.149-151)

> *As strange unto your town as to your talk,*
> *Who, every word by all my wit being scann'd,*
> *Wants wit in all one word to understand.*

Or stated more simply (4.3.21)

> *I understand thee not.*

In addition to issues of comprehension he seems to be experiencing 'time shifts' making him doubt his own perceptions (1.2.42-43)

> Ant.-S.: *How chance thou art return'd so soon?*
> Dro.-E.: *Returned so soon?*

Even though Antipholus-S. is in a city, like many others he has visited, he feels displaced (2.2.212-213)

> *Am I in earth, in heaven, or in hell?*
> *Sleeping or waking, mad or well advis'd?*

He is out of sync with what people are saying and doing and his experiences are beginning to match his fears of *"dark-working sorcerers that change the mind"* but he senses no ill will. On the contrary people take him to dinner (2.2.219), give him gifts (3.2.163-169), money (4.3.15) and generally treat him well (4.3.1-11).

Antipholus-S. also falls in love with what he believes is a witch but he doesn't care (3.2.39-40)

Are you a god? Would you create me new?

Transform me then, and to your power I'll yield.

Antipholus-S. yearns for transformation, he no longer wants to be the searching brother, he wants a new identity, he wants a lover, a family of his own, a home. Luciana represents the potential for all this to him.

Dromio-S. also thinks Ephesus is a place of transformation and discusses this with Antipholus-S. and Luciana (2.2.195-201)

Dro.-S.: *I am transformed, master, am I not?*

Ant.-S.: *I think thou art in mind, and so am I.*

Dro.-S.: *Nay, master, both in mind and in my shape.*

Ant.-S.: *Thou has thine own form.*

Dro.-S.: *No, I am an ape.* *

Luc.: *If thou art chang'd to aught, 'tis to an ass.*

Dro.-S.: *'Tis true, she rides me, and I long for grass;*

'Tis so, I am an ass.

(*ape in this instance could also mean a counterfeit or imitation of one's real self).

The ass is a powerful symbol and is used widely and in a variety of ways in this play. The ass motif, through sheer iteration, unifies the play and through its various meanings can be applied to almost all the characters at one time or another (Deborah Baker Wyrick, *The Ass Motif in 'The Comedy of Errors' and 'A Midsummer Night's Dream'*).

The general meanings of ass as ignorant fellow, fool, or conceited dolt can be applied to the various characters at various times since all are ignorant of what's going on or presume they have knowledge of a situation that they don't. In this way *The Comedy of Errors* generally describes the human condition prior to enlightenment.

The word ass could take on more specific meanings; for instance, through its Egyptian roots it can be associated with lust and take on 'priapic' (licentious) properties. It is in the context of 'licentious ass' that Adriana views her husband Antipholus-E. for she fears he is having an affair (2.1.104).

Ass could also be used as slang for 'woman' in the sense that they 'bear the sexual burden'. Associated meanings connected with ass such as 'beast of burden' and its use as a 'symbol of suffering' as well as its general meaning 'fool' help inform Adriana's comment that (2.1.14)

There's none but asses will be bridled so

a comment given in response to Luciana's chiding that a husband should be *"the bridle to your will"* (2.1.13).

In the context of transformation the ass has more specific associations. The picture of the ass as patiently bearing savage mistreatment as well as bearing its burden leads to the image of the animal as a type of Christ, an image that is reinforced by Christ's use of the ass for his triumphal entrance into Jerusalem (*Matthew* 21:5). Christ as the 'Cosmic Ass' patiently bearing man's burden of sin has led to portrayals of Christ in the guise of an ass. Christ, who rose from the dead, is himself a symbol of transformation.

In *The Comedy of Errors* the Dromios are cast as traditional fools who are repeatedly punished (through no fault of their own) and yet remain obedient and loyal to their masters (4.4.26-30)

I am an ass indeed; you may prove it by my
long ears. I have served him from the hour of my

> *nativity to this instant, and have nothing at his hands*
> *for my service but blows.*

They are the Christ-types and as such we can expect them to be a source of enlightenment in the play.

Shakespeare based *The Comedy of Errors* on two Roman plays but I would suggest other probable influences particularly with regards to the transformation theme. The first is by another Roman playwright, Apuleius, and his influential work *Metamorphosis,* better known as *The Golden Ass*. In it the main character, Lucius, is turned into an ass by magic and experiences the life of an ass with all its hardships and the constant threat of death. When Lucius hits rock bottom he reaches out to the goddess Isis for help. Out of respect he first washes himself in the sea and only then does he pray to Isis. He is granted a vision and from this vision his prayers are answered and he is returned to human form. Having been 'born again' he chooses to serve in the cult of Isis for his remaining years.

The situation is not unlike the one Antipholus-S. and Dromio-S. find themselves. Both have been transformed, both are perplexed and both are looking for deliverance (4.3.41-42)

> *And here we wander in illusions –*
> *Some blessed power deliver us from hence!*

Related to Apuleius' work is a work by Giordano Bruno called *Cabala del cavallo pegaseo* (*The Cabala of Pegasus*) and its annexed work *Asino cillenico* (*The Cillenican Ass*) both published in 1585 in England. Bruno's story makes explicit what Apuleius' story only implies. Bruno reveals how the human soul is no different than that of an ass's or any other living being. He does not shy away from the idea of Pythagorean metempsychosis (the transmission of a soul, usually at death, from one type of life form to another). In Bruno's story Onorio died on earth as an ass but was transmigrated into human form; upon each death he returned to heaven as the Pegasean Ass. Onorio remembers his past lives because, when in heaven, he only pretends to drink from the river Lethe (river of forgetfulness). By doing so he keeps the memory of his different lives intact.

Onorio discovers that all life is connected and that it shares in the same Spirit of God.

Shakespeare fully exploited these resources in *A Midsummer Night's Dream* but in *The Comedy of Errors* they lie in the subtext never rising above the idea that the ass is a symbol of Christ and that enlightenment follows transformation. Their imagery informs the story but they are not sources for its text. I do not wish to underplay the significance of the 'transformative ass' allusion; Shakespeare has intentionally introduced this idea just as he has intentionally moved his drama to Ephesus. These allusions are not introduced without understanding the meanings they carry; Shakespeare knew these works and the subtext is intentional; he wanted the associations made.

Enlightenment

The idea that transformation borders on enlightenment is seen in Adriana's anger with her husband. She first transforms him into a monster only to realize how much she loves him (4.2.19-22; 25; 28)

He is deformed, crooked, old and sere,
Ill-faced, worse bodied, shapeless everywhere;
Vicious, ungentle, foolish, blunt, unkind,
Stigmatical in making, worse in mind.
Ah, but I think him better than I say,
My heart prays for him, though my tongue do curse.

Transformations abound in the play. The Courtesan is transformed into Satan by Antipholus-S. and Dromio-S.'s fears (4.3.46-49)

Ant.-S.: Satan avoid, I charge thee tempt me not.

Dro.-S.: Master, is this mistress Satan?

Ant.-S.: It is the devil.

Dro.-S.: Nay, she is worse, she is the devil's dam.

Antipholus-E. is in turn transformed into a mad man by the Courtesan's imaginings (4.3.78-79; 83-85)

Now out of doubt Antipholus is mad,
Else would he never so demean himself;
The reason that I gather he is mad,
Besides this present instance of his rage,
Is a mad tale he told today at dinner.

This transformation, re-imagined by others, is attributed to demon possession (4.4.52)

...Satan hous'd within this man

as is the associated madness of Dromio (4.4.90)

Mistress, both man and master is possess'd.

It is the Abbess that begins to introduce some logic to the problem. She sees stress as the cause of Antipholus' antic behaviour, stress brought on by a jealous wife (5.1.85-86)

The consequence is then, thy jealous fits
Hath scar'd thy husband from the use of wits.

Adriana accepts her judgment, yet another epiphany (a type of self revelation), and sees the Abbess as only saying what she herself knew (5.1.90)

She did betray me to mine own reproof.

The Abbess plans to transform Antipholus from madness back to sanity (5.1.104-105)

With wholesome syrups, drugs and holy prayers,
To make of him a formal man again.

In truth, rest and prayer would be no more effective than the casting out of demons since the root cause of the problem is neither stress nor demons but a simple case of mistaken identity. Between the Abbess, Adriana, Luciana, Angelo, Egeon, and the Duke they manage to sort out the tale of the Antipholi and Dromios (5.1.387-388)

> *And I was ta'en for him, an he for me,*
> *And thereupon these errors are arose.*

With restoration of identity comes everyone's enlightenment; which brings us back to the last scene of the play and possible ways to interpret it.

Pentecost

The frame story and the comedy of errors converge where Egeon is to be executed: the place of doom. Symbolically this is the place and time of our death and the world we pass into is one of perfect knowledge, no longer looking through a 'glass darkly'.

In our play, like a stroke of lightning, everyone passes into this place of knowledge. They understand what has been happening and see the comical limits of their previous understanding.

Prior to death this type of epiphany can happen through the baptism of the Holy Spirit – an event celebrated in the Christian calendar as Pentecost. It was a holy day marking the descent of the Holy Ghost upon the apostles (*Acts* 2:1-4). This baptism with the Holy Ghost was repeated when St. Paul visited the Ephesians (*Acts* 19:1-6) and baptized them in the name of the Lord Jesus. To be baptized was to enter into a new life, to be reborn, to discover or rediscover your real identity.

The Comedy of Errors mentions Pentecost as a date (4.1.1)

> *You know since Pentecost the sum is due*

and later the Abbess invites all the parties to a *"gossips' feast"* (5.1.405). A gossips' feast was a baptismal feast set up for christenings.

To be baptized in the Holy Spirit was to be transformed into a new person; Saul the persecutor became Paul the apostle (*Acts* 9: 1-18, *Acts* 13: 9). In *The Comedy of Errors* the transformed characters find their true identities. To be baptized was to be baptized into the world of the spirit from the world of the flesh. It meant that the wall of partition separating people was broken down; bond man and free man do not exist in God's eyes, neither does male and female. Everyone is forgiven, everyone is welcome, all are fellow citizens of the household of God (*Ephesians* 2:11-19).

The play ends on this note of epiphany. Since the characters are entering into a baptismal feast we can assume that all will be transformed as a consequence of their reunification. We get a hint of what's in store for them with the last line of the play. Dromio-E. comments to his brother Dromio-S. (5.1.425-426)

We came into the world like brother and brother,
And now let's go hand in hand, not one before another.

Neither will take the title of elder or the status that goes with it. They claim instead equality. For a play littered with inequality this is a truly transformative event even if it starts at the bottom of the social ladder. Shakespeare does not tie up this comedy with pairings and re-pairings of couples even though that is clearly possible (Antipholus-E. with Adriana, Antipholus-S. with Luciana, Emilia with Egeon, Dromio-E. with Nell, Dromio-S. with Luce) instead he leads us into a baptismal feast. Families and people will be born again and new relationships will be forged.

Conclusion

The play begins with a man whose life is at risk, a family that is lost and divided, and a marriage that is close to divorce and ends with an act of mercy, re-unification of a family, and the hope of equity.

Unification is the theme of *The Comedy of Errors* and unity is the key to its understanding. Unity is the message given in the *Epistle to the Ephesians* (2:14)

For he is our peace, who hath made both one, and hath broken down the middle wall of partition between us.

It is also the message delivered in the last line of the play (5.1.425-426)

We came into the world like brother and brother,
And now let's go hand in hand, not one before another.

This unity is also apparent when we look at the characters in the play. They complete each other; they balance each other. The strong headed, independent Adriana is balanced by the submissive, obedient Luciana. And the role of women in marriage is balanced by the women who exist outside of marriage, the Courtesan and the Abbess.

Opposite/balancing natures can also be seen in the twin Antipholi. Antipholus-E. is a confident businessman who has placed his career over his family while Antipholus-S. is a man currently in doubt who gave up his career to find his missing family.

The Antipholi are as Adriana/Luciana are, two sides of the same coin. It is, in part, Shakespeare's approach to playwriting; creating differing world views that can embody each character and give them a unique voice. Each stock type acting as a skeleton that a personality is built upon, each given their own perspective to add a richness to their dialogue and simultaneously allow Shakespeare to explore the many aspects of our humanity. This simultaneity does not just exist with characters it also exists in the structure of the play. Shakespeare has taken the bones of two Plautine comedies and saturated them with biblical references. He did this by matching characters and situations from the different sources; for example, he took the Plautine law separating foreigners from citizens and permeated it with allusions to biblical texts about similar laws. He conflates and combines his sources verbally and with shared imagery.

He has also cleverly exploited terms from the business/material world that do double duty in the spiritual world. This allows for verbal linkages and double meanings; for example, consider words like angels, debt, redemption and forgiveness. This punning is indicative of the play's structure. Two meanings compete for the same space in our understanding but because both are relevant and intentional the play evades a simple explanation and rather opts for two simultaneously.

This method creates the unity we perceive in *The Comedy of Errors* and ties in with its theme. The characters adopt different roles but a balanced argument is put forth through their cumulative contributions. The plot drives the play to its conclusion while the arguments get focused to their more balanced positions as the more extreme outliers expose their tragic underpinnings.

Bibliography

1) *The Comedy of Errors*, W. Shakespeare, edited by R.A. Foakes, The Arden Shakespeare, 3rd series, Cengage Learning, 2007.
2) *'Were it not against our laws': oppression and resistance in Shakespeare's 'Comedy of Errors'*, Eric Heinze, *Legal Studies*, Vol. 29 No. 2, June 2009, p.230-263.
3) *The Madness of Syracusan Antipholus*, Robert Viking O'Brien, *Early Modern Literary Studies*, 2.1 (1996): 3.1-26.
4) *The Ass Motif in 'The Comedy of Errors' and 'A Midsummer Night's Dream'*, Deborah Baker Wyrick, *Shakespeare Quarterly*, Vol. 33, No. 4 (Winter, 1982), p. 432-448.
5) *Logic Versus the Slovenly World in Shakespearean Comedy*, O.B. Hardison Jr., *Shakespeare Quarterly*, Vol. 31, No. 3 (Autumn, 1980), p.311-322.
6) *Elder and Younger: The Opening Scene of 'The Comedy of Errors'*, Patricia Parker, *Shakespeare Quarterly*, Vol. 34, No. 3 (Autumn, 1983), p. 325-327.
7) *Shakespeare from the Margins: language, culture, context*, Patricia Parker, Chapter 2, The Bible and the Marketplace: *The Comedy of Errors*, p. 56-83, University of Chicago Press, 1996.
8) *The Cabala of Pegasus*, Giordano Bruno, translated and annotated by Sidney L. Sondergard and Madison U. Sowell, Yale University Press, New Haven and London, 2002.
9) *Metamorphoses* (Book I-VI), Apuleius, translated by J. Arthur Hanson, Harvard University Press, 2001.
10) *Metamorphoses* (Book VII-XI), Apuleius, translated by J. Arthur Hanson, Harvard University Press, 2001.
11) *The Holy Bible*, King James Version, Zondervan Publishing House, 1962.

The Merry Wives of Windsor: [Alt/Shift/Control]

Introduction

The Merry Wives of Windsor is a comedy about women's power set against a backdrop of a changing English society. The mercantile town of Windsor reflects a society in flux where the middle class, through their accumulation of wealth, is able to exert control over those possessing title who traditionally wield the power. This changing power dynamic echoes through the society and we see female wit establish itself as a tool that can be used as a means of competing with both traditional male and parental control. In this society money can invert inherited privilege and cleverness can invert traditional values.

The major threat to the stability of this emerging mercantile meritocracy is a figure from the traditional English upper class. He comes in the form of a corrupt knight by the name of Falstaff. It is his presence and gift for translation (in that he translates the women and is in turn translated by them) that acts as a catalyst to reveal the many meanings to be found in *The Merry Wives of Windsor*.

Alternative power and shifting control are hallmarks in *The Merry Wives of Windsor*. It is a drama that profiles specifically middle class wives and the shifting power dynamics both in the home and in society. It was written during the reign of Queen Elizabeth I, a powerful woman and a contradictory figure. She legitimized female authority (at a time when it was questioned) by supporting a traditional social hierarchy. By doing so traditional society was in turn obliged to defend her claim to power.

In *The Merry Wives of Windsor* we find a similar situation where female power is exercised over men in order to preserve and perpetuate the conservative institution of marriage. There is an irony or an inversion in this in that the most liberal ideas are enlisted in order to support the most conservative institutions of that society. This process of inversion can be seen to operate on many levels throughout the play.

Enter the Cuckoo

The Merry Wives of Windsor can be called a middle class drama in that it profiles and draws from this stratum of society its main characters; it's a merchants' drama where the merchants are preoccupied with the safeguarding of property and expanding their privilege. They are the new moneyed class but without any pedigree.

The play begins with a poaching; Falstaff has killed Shallow's deer (his property) and invaded his hunting lodge (1.1.104-105)

Knight, you have beaten my men, kill'd my
deer and broke open my lodge.

Falstaff is a knight, one of the upper crust, who has wasted any wealth he possessed. He is now suffering hard times and is looking for any means to shore up his financial position. Falstaff is challenging Shallow's social rank (who is a member of the middle class) by poaching his deer (see Jeffrey Theis). He is also challenging Shallow's ability to protect his own property. Shallow retaliates by threatening to take Falstaff to court (1.1.1-2)

I will make a Star
Chamber matter of it.

Although hunting rights and privileges afforded the elite were much different than what we would consider as just in our day, Shallow does believe that Falstaff has exceeded his rights and represents a threat to social order. George Page (another member of the middle class) hopes to resolve this issue and mediate the dispute by inviting the warring parties into his home. He in fact does arrange a settlement (which we the audience are not privy to) and all parties sit down to share in a dinner of venison the *"ill killed"* deer that was the subject of the unpleasantness.

Page hopes that the bad behaviour ends here but in fact he has invited the fat cuckoo into his own nest for it is here, over dinner, that Falstaff makes the acquaintance of both Mistress Page and Mistress Ford, the subjects of his future poaching.

It is in this first Act that Falstaff is revealed for the subversive character that he is. Falstaff is a destabilizing influence, an ill angel, who infects societies and discredits their most noble institutions. His petty thievery discredits his knighthood but it is just one instance of his more general 'modus operandi' which is to subvert all institutions for his own personal gain. He is the embodiment of the acquisitive cuckoo and equally destructive.

It is following this dinner that Falstaff schemes (1.3.40-42)

I do mean to make love to

Ford's wife. I spy entertainment in her: she discourses,

she carves, she gives the leer of invitation.

His plan is to seduce the wife to get access to the husband's purse (1.3.49-50)

Now, the report goes she has all the rule of

her husband's purse: he hath a legion of angels.

It is a plan he hopes to duplicate (1.3.55-57)

I have writ me here a letter to her; and here

another to Page's wife, who even now gave me good

eyes too, examined my parts with most judicious

oeillades.

Neither their marriages nor his own lust enters into the equation; he is strictly scheming for their money (1.3.66-67)

I will be cheaters

to them both, and they shall be exchequers to me.

The institution he violates is irrelevant to him, the people or their status equally so, all that matters to Falstaff is the chance at possible gain. He is an egalitarian con man.

Money Goes Before

The early portion of the play has introduced us to two gentlemen of the higher class, Falstaff and Fenton, both of whom are suffering hard times because of their wasteful excesses. These are gentlemen 'made cheap' who, stripped of their money, are forced to actively woo a hierarchically lower class in order to poach their wealth. Both men plan to enrich themselves at the expense of this lower class. Falstaff hopes to seduce the wives of two wealthy merchants (Frank Ford and George Page) in order to gain access to their purses and Fenton hopes to marry Anne Page (George's daughter) also in hopes of gaining access to her family's fortune, something he has openly admitted to Anne herself (3.4.13-14)

Albeit I will confess thy father's wealth
Was the first motive that I wooed thee, Anne.

Money has made permeable the rigid class system that previously would not have entertained such relationships. Monetary priority has over-turned a status system previously conceived as rigid and unchanging (2.2.160)

for they say if money go before, all ways do lie open.

Patricia Parker (*Shakespeare from the Margins*, Chapter 1) believes this mobility has now introduced a confusion as to what is prior and what comes after because wealth is taking precedence over title and quietly questioning traditional advantage. The play reflects these shifting values by showing several characters that can no longer understand the concept of precedence. For instance Slender inverts successors for ancestors (1.1.12-13)

> *All his successors - gone before him - hath*
> *done't; and all his ancestors - that come after him - may.*

It is an inversion that consistently occurs throughout the play (1.1.229-231)

> *I will marry her, sir, at your request. But if*
> *there be no great love in the beginning, yet heaven may*
> *decrease it upon better acquaintance.*

This inability to tell what comes before from what comes after is used for humorous effect but it suggests a society that is undergoing change, one that is using money as an egalitarian tool to lay bare the structures that give rise to priority and order. Money/wealth is being used to question the very basis of a hierarchy.

Money is not the only tool of inversion used in the play for we also see wit employed by the women to get the upper hand over controlling and conniving men. In addition we witness children out-maneuver their parents' wishes in order to achieve their own love-match, one where the girl chooses the boy. Women controlling men and children outwitting parents are the stock and trade of comedies; what is seen as normal in society is inverted. In this instance it shows us the evolving world view of a society in flux. Money can invert privilege and wit can invert control.

All this occurs in a society that despite these inversions appears to function completely normally, and the reason for this is that wit is linked with virtue and control with kindness; change occurs responsibly.

Being Translated

Patricia Parker (*Shakespeare from the Margins*, Chapter 4) argues that *The Merry Wives of Windsor* is a play that is conceptually centered on the idea of 'translation' and its many meanings while Jeffrey Theis believes that it is the concept of 'poaching' which is pivotal, when used in its most general and metaphorical sense as the usurpation of a person's control over property or people. Parker's argument arises from a network of wordplay that occurs throughout the comedy that is all based on the expanding meanings of the word 'translate' while Theis bases his related idea of poaching on documents that were written at the time (such as John Manwood's *Treatise and Discourse of the Laws of the Forrests*, 1598) which described the forest and game laws of England and their distinctly political nature.

Both works help elucidate *The Merry Wives of Windsor* but because translation can include such meanings as the translation of property from one owner to another, i.e. stealing or poaching; and because the word poaching was never used in any of Shakespeare's works it is justifiable to name 'translation' as the KEY WORD in the play. As Parker suggests 'translate' unifies the play's puns and wordplay while at the same time justifies the inclusion of the Latin lesson (4.1) a scene that is often deleted or deemed as inconsequential to the play's action. Theis' insights are also of importance for the symbolism of the deer and its associated poaching is a strong and recurrent idea that fills the play's pages with 'buck' imagery. Both concepts can be considered to be dilating ideas in that they expand from their first mention and bleed into the entire play informing its content and giving rise to its images, as such both concepts will be explored.

Translate, to define the word in more detail, can mean transporting or translating words from one language into another; to render meaning. It can also mean to move, bear or carry an object from one place to another (like a man in a basket). The word can also imply the conveying of property from one owner to another legally or illegally as in stealing (stealing being Nim's, Pistol's and Bardolph's expertise). Translate can also mean to express in other terms, to explain or convert, to retransmit or paraphrase. This is Mistress Quickly's particular gift and it is demonstrated in the Latin lesson where she translates Latin into the literal vulgar tongue i.e. obscenity. Falstaff is also skilled in a similar art in that he can translate looks into dishonest intensions. Translate can also mean to transform, in that people can be translated into stags. Curiously translate was also an early modern term for metaphor encompassing the concept of translating from the literal to the figurative. It is through these many meanings that the term helps unify the play and connect disparate scenes.

The Latin lesson (4.1) gives us an indication of what fun one can have with the concept of translation. In this scene instead of finding a typical Latin lesson where a student translates out of Latin into English and back into Latin we have instead a lesson conducted by a Welsh teacher (who mispronounces) for a school boy (who doesn't understand) in the presence of an interfering Mistress Quickly. Quickly is horrified as she miscomprehends the Latin for poorly pronounced English slang (*'pulcher'* becomes *'polecats'* or prostitutes to Mistress Quickly's ears (4.1.23-24)). It is her continuing interference that prevents the Latin from returning to Latin in that she allows it to escape into meanings that were never intended.

This scene, devoted to translation, is typical of the rest of the play. Differing acts of translation are involved in most scenes but they escape their expected interpretation and instead follow one of their variant meanings; initial intentions are never realized. To put it simply this is not a play about honest translation (1.3.46-47)

> *He hath studied her well and translated her will*
> *— out of honesty into English.*

Falstaff's Translations

Falstaff conceives of the idea to exploit Mistress Page and Mistress Ford when he translates their behaviour into words of desire. Just as Latin was turned into English (Englished) he turns behaviour into English (1.3.42-45)

> *I can construe*
> *the action of her familiar style, and the hardest*
> *voice of her behaviour - to be Englished rightly - is:*
> *'I am Sir John Falstaff's'.*

By translating her behaviour he hopes to translate her form. Falstaff wishes to make Mistress Ford his lover and then change her into her husband's purse from which he will translate Ford's wealth to himself (1.3.49-50)

> *Now, the report goes she has all the rule of*
> *her husband's purse: he hath a legion of angels.*

Pistol also points out that Falstaff has translated Mistress Ford's will out of honesty and into English i.e. he has changed her honesty into something he can understand (1.3.46-47).

Falstaff's inability to understand or appreciate honest behaviour is what makes Falstaff Falstaff. He is a narcissist incapable of any behaviour that does not benefit himself. Deceit is his language of choice and deceit is what he understands in others. When Frank Ford, who translates himself into Master Brook (2.1.193-194), approaches him with a deal to seduce 'Ford's wife' it is a bargain he can understand - it is despicable on all levels and primarily beneficial to himself (2.2.180-271).

Interestingly in this play we have a seduction without lust (for Falstaff is only interested in the wives' money) and a marriage without love (for Ford does not trust his wife). Ford is primarily concerned with his property and with its theft or depreciation (2.2.276-278)

> *See the hell of having a false woman: my*

> *bed shall be abused, my coffers ransacked, my*
> *reputation gnawn at*

for along with adultery comes adulteration (another form of translation) when that which is pure is rendered impure.

When Pistol and Nim warn Frank Ford and George Page of Falstaff's plans for their wives Page dismisses the idea outright but Ford becomes obsessed by it. Thievery (and this is a type of thievery) runs throughout the multiple plots of the comedy. We see it in Falstaff's poaching, in Pistol and Nim's pilfering and in Ford's worries over his coffers. But to steal is merely to move an object form one place to another i.e. to translate or convey (1.3.26-27)

> *'Convey', the wise call it. 'Steal'? Foh!*
> *A fico for the phrase!*

Falstaff is acquisitive; he translates other people's properties to himself. It is this impulse that drives him in his attempts to translate Ford's and Page's wives for his own consumption. But Falstaff not only translates he himself is also the subject of translation. When the wives receive identical letters of seduction from him they plan revenge or more precisely they plan to 'translate or render' Falstaff with their revenge (2.1.56-60)

> *What tempest, I trow, threw this*
> *whale, with so many tuns of oil in his belly, ashore at*
> *Windsor? How shall I be revenged on him? I think the*
> *best way were to entertain him with hope, till the*
> *wicked fire of lust have melted him in his own grease.*

This scene plays on the fact that another word for translate is 'to render', i.e., to render a word into another language; but of course render also means 'to melt' as fat into oil. We find that Falstaff is both rendered and translated in keeping with the wives' plans. This occurs when Frank

Ford returns unexpectedly while Falstaff is in the early stages of courting his wife. Alice Ford is warned by Margaret Page (3.3.107-108)

> *but if you have a friend*
> *here, convey, convey him out*

and again (3.3.116-117)

> *Your husband's here at hand:*
> *bethink you of some conveyance.*

Falstaff is to be loaded in a buck-basket and translated or conveyed out of the house and down to the river. Falstaff speaks of his own rendering (3.5.103-107)

> *to be stopped in like a strong distillation with stinking*
> *clothes that fretted in their own grease. Think of that,*
> *a man of my kidney, think of that - that am as subject*
> *to heat as butter - a man of continual dissolution and*
> *thaw.*

This is not yet the end of Falstaff's trials for the women, though happy with the outcome, do not yet feel compensated for the effrontery they have endured (3.3.175-176; 180-181)

> *we will*
> *yet have more tricks with Falstaff...*
> *give him another hope, to betray him to*
> *another punishment.*

Presumption about their character has given them reason for revenge. Both Falstaff and Frank Ford have disrespected their characters by thinking them wanton women and both will be made to suffer for it.

In Falstaff's second misadventure the wives conspire to dress him as a woman, *"the fat woman of Brainford"* (4.2.71-72) or more precisely *"the witch of Brainford"* (4.2.93). Falstaff's transformation or translation into a woman is essential in his escape because Master Ford is intent on looking for him in every Freudian nook and cranny (3.5.136-138)

> *But, lest the*
> *devil that guides him should aid him, I will search*
> *impossible places.*

These places include the chimney (where they discharge their birding-pieces), kiln-hole (or kill-hole: an opening in the oven), press (large cupboard), coffer, chest, trunk, well, vault and every such yonic place in the house. Ford's mania is noted by his friends and they try to reason with him (4.2.147-150)

> Evans: *Master Ford, you must pray, and not follow the*
> *imaginations of your own heart: this is jealousies.*
> Ford: *Well, he's not here I seek for.*
> Page: *No, nor nowhere else but in your brain.*

Ford's imaginings are the source of his troubles and Shakespeare highlights this by naming the witch *'Brainford'* to show she is the manifestation of Ford's own worst thoughts. Ford is afraid of being cuckolded but he is also afraid of witchcraft (4.2.162-163; 166-167)

> *A witch, a quean, an old cozening quean! Have I*
> *not forbid her my house?*
> *She works by charms, by spells, by the figure, and such*
> *daubery as this is, beyond our element.*

The wives use this phobia against him by dressing Falstaff as the old woman of Brainford. This gives Ford two reasons to eject *'Mother Prat'* from his house; first he cannot abide witchcraft, second he has explicitly forbid her from his house. Ford, who feels he has lost control of his wife, leaps at the chance to have control over something and exercises his will by forcibly ejecting Brainford from his world.

Having gotten Falstaff beaten *'unpitifully'* and having humiliated Frank Ford in front of his peers the wives agree that it is now time to tell the husbands what they have done to Falstaff and why. They also hope this will put Frank Ford's mind finally at ease (4.2.204-205)

> *Yes, by all means, if it be but to scrape*
> *the figures out of your husband's brains.*

While the affront is still fresh in everyone's minds the wives, in conjunction with their husbands, plan one final and this time public shaming of Falstaff. Falstaff, the man they have translated in a basket, transformed into a witch, is now to be changed into a deer (4.2.212-213)

> *Come, to the forge with it, then shape*
> *it: I would not have things cool.*

The final shaming involves the entire community for Falstaff has shown himself to be a public nuisance. The play has been compared to a 'skimmington' by Anne Parten and this last scene to a 'witches sabbath' by Nancy Cotton and there are certainly elements of both in its structure. The scene for Falstaff's final translation or transformation takes place in Windsor forest and it features a cast drawn from town folk and their children. It is to be a community event but it is staged as an assignation between lovers (hence its dual nature as skimmington/sabbath). The wives lure Falstaff to one more meeting in the hope of amourous pleasure. He is to meet them at midnight dressed as Herne the hunter (4.4.39-44)

> *Marry, this is our device:*
> *That Falstaff at that oak shall meet with us,*
> *Disguised like Herne, with huge horns on his head.*

The wives are acting like witches in that they transubstantiate or translate a man into a beast (like Circe in *The Odyssey*). The deer or stag was the Renaissance symbol for lust and an appropriate symbol for Falstaff who now fancies himself a Jove (5.5.2-4)

> *Now the hot-blooded gods assist me!*
> *Remember Jove, thou wast a bull for thy Europa: love*
> *set on thy horns.*

This Falstaff is ready for rutting and offers himself to the two ladies (5.5.12; 24)

> *I am here a Windsor stag...*
> *Divide me like a bribed buck, each a haunch.*

So in this early part of this final scene there is the sinister hint of a witches' sabbath but it exists mainly in Falstaff's imagination. He is here as a horned creature to engage in an orgy with these Windsor wives, in these Windsor woods, at the midnight hour, beneath Jove's oak (5.2.12-13)

> *No man means evil but*
> *the devil, and we shall know him by his horns.*

It is appropriate that Falstaff wears the cuckold's horns in this play because he is the man rendered impotent by female betrayal and who is outsmarted by them three times. His male power is lost to their female dominance, but it is a dominance exercised in the preservation of their honest reputations, something Falstaff was trying to strip them of. The wives' tricks have preserved both their reputations as well as their husbands' by ensuring that their marriages be placed beyond the pale of gossip. They have in fact protected the community by revealing and rejecting the acquisitive cuckoo (5.3.21-22)

> *Against such lewdsters and their lechery*
> *Those that betray them do no treachery.*

The Skimmington

The folk ritual known as the skimmington was an expression of a community's disapproval of certain behaviours. It could be used to humiliate adulterers but it could also be used to expose controlling women and their ineffective or cuckolded husbands. The purpose of a skimmington was to call attention to an unwanted behaviour, circumscribe it and use collective laughter to drive it away.

A skimmington procession would often have the offender (such as a cuckolded husband) mounted backwards on an ass while being paraded about town to the accompaniment of pounding kitchen implements. Often a woman's smock would be carried as a banner hanging from a staff that was crowned with deer horns.

The traditional skimmington shows a thematic affinity with but not a direct correspondence to *The Merry Wives of Windsor*. They share a common imagery but serve different purposes. In *Merry Wives* it is not the powerful women that are a threat to the community but rather the perverting presence of Falstaff. The women preserve and conserve while Falstaff subverts.

Falstaff is shown to be an ineffectual male and subject to the control of women but it is at the hands of virtuous women beyond reproach. Falstaff becomes symbolic of the true cuckold and rightly the subject of the skimmington but the controlling women are exempt from any wrong doing.

The three tricks played on Falstaff by the wives are all forms of emasculation; when he is dumped into the Thames as something foul which must be cleaned Mistress Quickly tells him it was because the servants *"mistook their erection"* (3.5.37-38) to which Falstaff replies *"so did I mine"*. In the second trick he is made to adopt a sexual disguise by dressing and acting as a woman, and in the final trick the women *"dishorn"* (4.4.62) his spirit.

There is an imagistic drift between the play and a skimmington in that they share the same elements. The wives, like in a true skimmington, dunk the adulterer in a pond. The wives dress Falstaff in a woman's frock just like the smock that acts as a banner in a skimmington and finally they make him wear the deer horns of a cuckold. The common elements appear in different contexts but constitute a shared imagery.

Rendering Justice

In *The Merry Wives of Windsor* the dispensing of justice takes place on an intimate scale. It is often accomplished between the disputing parties and a few arbiters, neither the courts nor the church is brought into the disputes even though representatives of each (Judge Shallow and Pastor Evans) are present. The arguments are settled within the community according to community standards. In the play several disputes stand out; the first is between Shallow and Falstaff over the poached deer, second is the duel between Caius and Evans, third is between Fred Ford and his wife, fourth is between Anne Page and her parents, and fifth is between Falstaff and the women. All the disputes revolve around the idea of control and all the disputes are resolved informally with a gentleness of spirit and a forgiving attitude where punishments are tailored to fit the crime.

Page, Evans, and the Host arbitrate the Shallow/Falstaff complaint (1.1.127-131) by having the warring parties sit down to a dinner of the ill-killed deer where they share in its eating (1.1.180-182). The Host arbitrates the duel between Caius and Evans (1.4.109-110) (2.1.185-187) (2.3) (3.1), a dispute founded on a misunderstanding and resolves it though a series of misdirections. Fred Ford's dispute with his wife is partially arbitrated by his peers who shame him for his unfounded suspicions (4.2.144-150) but it is his wife that finally forgives him after due penance (4.4.6-9). It is once again the Host that assists Fenton in Anne's dispute with her parents (4.6) but it is the parents' good nature that finally allows for the acceptance of their daughter's judgment (5.5.230-231; 233-234).

The major dispute of the play is of a more malevolent and wide ranging nature and so requires the community as a whole to come together to publicly shame Falstaff for his presumption and boundary issues. It is an act intended to both identify and ostracize a public threat. Falstaff fears such a public 'outing' and worries about it (4.5.88-91)

> *If it should come to*
> *the ear of the court how I have been transformed, and*
> *how my transformation hath been washed and cudgelled,*
> *they would melt me out of my fat drop by drop.*

But the possibility of a shaming is not however a strong enough deterrent; with little inducement Falstaff is once again ready to have a liaison with the women. This only goes to confirm how incorrigible the fat knight is. It is clear in this case that the private punishments carried out by the women have not worked and that a public shaming is required to put an end to his antics.

The public mocking will mark him as an object of derision and make him the butt of jokes. Any power or authority he possessed will be lost (4.4.61-63)

> *The truth being known,*
> *We'll all present ourselves, dishorn the spirit,*
> *And mock him home to Windsor.*

The Imaginative Landscape

The play opened with a deer hunting scene (Falstaff poaching a deer) and closes with a deer hunting scene (Falstaff as the deer being hunted by the community) (5.5.12-13)

> *I am here a Windsor stag, and the fattest, I*
> *think, i'the forest.*

This final scene takes place in a forest but it is really the world of the imagination (Falstaff's hopes and fears) based on myths and 'old wives tales' common to everyone's upbringing. Falstaff hopes he is Jove, the transforming serial seducer (5.5.2-4)

> *Now the hot-blooded gods assist me!*

> *Remember, Jove, thou wast a bull for thy Europa: love*
> *set on thy horns*

but instead he is to find out he is the focus of a skimmington and subject to his own childhood fears.

Wendy Wall provides us with an informative glimpse into the fairy stories associated with childhood and their caregivers. She presents fairy stories as a type of obsolete knowledge that was relegated to the domain of females where it could be used to coerce children into obedience (much like religion's use of fire and brimstone). These stories were felt to infiltrate all classes because they were perpetuated by childhood nurses who were drawn from the working class and assisted in the raising of the upper class. Childhood being the one stage of development permeable to cross class contamination. All social groups share in this common knowledge of fairy lore. Belief in this imaginative world is held in a greater or lesser degree by one's subsequent upbringing and proclivity to superstition.

Falstaff falls victim to this fairy world, a world he is translated into by his over active imagination, when he is momentarily caught off guard. He is surprised in a private moment; his seduction is interrupted and his orgy mates flee at the sight of a childhood fear: punishing fairies. Falstaff flinches, he knows they have frightened him, and when he is confronted he is a good enough sport to acknowledge it (5.5.119; 121-126)

> *I do begin to perceive that I am made an ass.*
> *And these are not fairies. I was three or four*
> *times in the thought they were not fairies, and yet the*
> *guiltiness of my mind, the sudden surprise of my*
> *powers, drove the grossness of the foppery into a*
> *received belief...that they were fairies.*

William Carroll points out in his essay how the power of the imagination can shape and transform one's reality. Falstaff has previously shown himself to be highly dependent on his imagination for he possesses a deluded image of himself. He sees himself as a Don Juan type, an Adonis, capable of seducing the wives and manipulating their purses. The fact that Falstaff is hanging onto reality by a thread makes it even more believable that he could fall for such a theatrical, though carefully organized, trick. But Falstaff is not the only imaginatively active character in the play, so too is Frank Ford. Ford is the only other person in the play that considers Falstaff to be capable of seducing his wife. Just as Falstaff is self deluded so is Ford but Ford's deception is induced by jealousy instead of vanity.

Ford's paranoia consumes him and his reason. He is made a puppet to his worst fears (5.5.126-127)

See now how wit may be
made a Jack-a-Lent when 'tis upon ill employment!

Ford and Falstaff, besides sharing the delusion of Falstaff's seductive powers, also believe that the women are loose based on their merry humour. This was not an uncommon belief in the 16th century that of equating levity of spirit with levity of morals. Anne Parten points out this implied belief by highlighting the fact that Mistress Page worries about this when considering how she might have led Falstaff on (2.1.22-23)

I was then frugal
of my mirth.

So the campaign against Falstaff is not only over presumption but it is also in defense of the concept of feminine mirth (4.2.100-101)

Wives may be merry and yet honest too.
We do not act that often jest and laugh.

Ford and Falstaff both employ a chain of reasoning that sees feminine mirth as a forerunner to feminine adultery and therefore a precursor to cuckoldry. Both men have violated the Garter Motto (*Honi soit qui mal y pense*; shamed be he who thinks evil of it) by seeing evil where there was none and both men will be shamed for it.

Ford is shamed in front of his peers for having such a suspicious nature and for suspecting such a blameless wife. His mind is finally put to ease by his wife who explains all that had happened and all that they did to punish Falstaff. Ford's humiliation serves as his penance.

Falstaff's shaming had to be more public since the danger he represented was so much the greater. Falstaff's lack of boundaries made him a public danger and so his exposure was required to bring him to heel. A con man can only be allowed to remain in a society when everyone knows he is a con man and so none are subject to his deceptions. So like a poisonous plant Falstaff can be safely enjoyed without putting anyone at risk only if he is effectively side-lined by his public exposure.

Stories and Backstories
a) Mistress Quickly

Mistress Quickly is the main carrier, translator, and mover of messages in the play. She is the major go-between and carries messages between Falstaff and the wives as well as between Anne Page and all her suitors (Slender, Caius, and Fenton). To carry is of course to convey or to transport or to translate from one place to another. It is a term used repeatedly throughout the play and not just with reference to Mistress Quickly.

Mistress Quickly is referred to as '*she-Mercury*' (2.2.76) with reference to the fact that Mercury was the messenger of the gods. But Mercury was a translator on many levels; he was also a thief (as an infant he stole Apollo's heifers) and was known as the patron to thieves. Mercury was also credited with inventing the written language and through his eloquence and persuasiveness became the ideal businessmen and patron to the mercantile industry. Mercury's positive aspects are seen in trade and commerce but Mercury was also known to cross moral boundaries where his interest with profit of any kind, lawful or unlawful, tied him into the world of gambling and con men (cozeners) and established him as the god of cunning.

Quickly's role is marginal but her symbolism is monumental for here we have a play steeped in concerns over property, language, theft, and commerce. It is a merchant's drama filled with translations of every type. To say that Mercury lies at the very heart of the drama would not be an understatement.

Mercury by tradition was regarded as the leader of the Graces (this is why he appears in Boticelli's *Primavera*) which in turn represented 'concord in opposition'. This may help explain Quickly's final role as Queen of the Fairies where she leads the community against the threat posed by Falstaff. Concord in opposition was an idea representing ordered change, it recalled the ratcheting that goes on between opposing forces and the harmony of balance that can be achieved in their resolution. The forces of ordered change are uniting against the excessive threat symbolized by Falstaff's anarchy.

b) Falstaff

Falstaff is the most dangerous character in the comedy in that he preys on others and is no respecter of boundaries. If Mistress Quickly is the messenger part of Mercury then Falstaff is the dark side, the gambler, the con man, the thief. He is the man seeking unlawful profit. He is the cuckoo who is invited into the positive world of middle class merchants and who returns their kindness with a conspiracy to seduce their wives. Falstaff's plan, as he sees it, is thrift through thievery (1.3.39-41)

> *but I am now about no waste: I*
> *am about thrift. Briefly, I do mean to make love to*

Ford's wife.

Falstaff is designed to evoke several classical figures as diverse as Actaeon, Jove, Bacchus, Silenus, and Lucius (from Apuleius' *The Golden Ass*). He is a four part animal - goat, stag, ass, and ox - a figure of mythological excess.

His association with the ass and ox is the easiest to understand. It comes from an allusion to *Deuteronomy* (5:21)

Neither shalt thou desire thy neighbour's wife, neither shalt thou covet thy neighbour's house, his field, or his manservant, or his maidservant, his ox, or his ass, or anything that is thy neighbour's.

This reference is made in association with Falstaff's confession and Ford's response (5.5.119-120)

Fal.: *I do begin to perceive that I am made an ass.*

Ford: *Ay, and an ox too: both the proofs are extant.*

Ford is accusing Falstaff of coveting and, by association, two other closely related sins, those of theft and adultery.

Falstaff is the perfect comic villain in that he poses a real threat to the community but lacks the ability to succeed. Because of this the menace he poses becomes an amusing diversion.

Jeanne Addison Roberts sees Falstaff as witty but also self deluded. He is a source of conflicting signals. When he sends identical letters of seduction to the wives we view him as outrageously presumptuous but through the tone of the letters, through their bluntness, he becomes comically appealing.

Falstaff's actions are often made more comic by their juxtaposition with more serious events such as when Falstaff is to act as a gigolo for 'Mr. Brook'. His actions can be seen as harmless and preposterous especially when compared to Ford's own scheme to trap and humiliate his wife. Falstaff, the villain, is made more sympathetic when presented using these techniques.

Falstaff is often presented as a ridiculous threat but a charming person. We see this when Falstaff, the would-be adulterer, is loaded into a buck basket. The event pushes the limits of comedy but to have the same man describe it while drowning his sorrows evokes a sense of pathos.

Falstaff, who fancied himself Jove, is forced over the course of the play to see himself as mortal. Bacchus, one of the few dying gods, can be seen in this realization. Bacchus, who was known for the danger, chaos and unexpected that accompanied him, who subverted the oppressive restraint of the powerful, becomes reduced to Silenus his drunken sidekick.

Falstaff by the end of the play represents the 'deceiver deceived'. Dressed in a fine set of deer horns the man who set out to cuckold Ford and Page finds he is the true cuckold having been outsmarted by the women.

The Actaeon myth is mentioned several times in the play and Falstaff's journey echoes it effectively; he is changed into a '*fat Windsor stag*' through his dealing with the wives. Just as Actaeon was changed into a stag when he viewed naked Diana, Falstaff meets a similar fate through his hopes of seducing the wives but instead of being eaten by his hounds he is merely exposed for the threat he is.

Falstaff can also be viewed as a scapegoat. Although he is definitely guilty of that which he is accused others in the play are also culpable of similar, though minor, offenses. George Page is presumptuous of his station, he acts like an aristocrat (by owning hunting hounds and entertaining his betters), and harbours hopes that by adopting the manners of the elite he might rise to their social position. His daughter, Anne, is equally presumptuous. She regards her judgment to be superior to her parents and so subverts her parent's prerogative to choose a husband for her and instead decides to choose her own. The wives are also presumptuous in that they feel no need to inform their husbands about the schemes they will enact against Falstaff. They feel their honour is their concern. They assume the role of their own protectors.

All these characters are exceeding the limitations normally prescribed to their social position or sex. They are all grasping for power and control not normally in their purview but the characters do so virtuously. They intend no harm. This is not the case with Falstaff; his acts are all advantageous to himself and are capable of harming others. He represents a clear danger that must be identified. By scapegoating Falstaff the society may hope to excise the darker aspects that come with exercising control over another's power or property. The community is saying you are 'free to aspire' so long as you do no harm but that you are not 'free to conspire' against others in that you cannot take from or harm another by your actions.

Disruption to the status quo is the means people employ to change customs. As long as these transgressions pose a limited threat they are allowed. The community can clearly accept all the disruptions except Falstaff's. He has exceeded the permissible 'ratcheting' a changing society permits and is punished for it. Falstaff is however not ostracized; like the alluded-to prodigal (4.5.7) he is still a welcomed part of the community (5.5.168-170)

> *Yet be cheerful, knight: thou shalt eat a posset*
> *tonight at my house, where I will desire thee to laugh*
> *at my wife that now laughs at thee.*

Falstaff is a figure of excess and as such he needs to be feared. He knows no limit. His transgressions will continue if not checked. The wives believe they have quenched his desire after his second humiliation (4.2.198-199)

> *The spirit of wantonness is sure scared*
> *out of him*

but it only takes a message from Mistress Quickly to stir his plans afresh (5.1.1-2)

> *Go, I'll hold: this*
> *is the third time - I hope good luck lies in odd numbers.*

It is Falstaff's ever optimistic brand of delusion and abundance of appetite that makes him such a threat.

Frederick Jonassen makes an interesting argument when he likens Falstaff's encounter with the Windsor wives to the tradition of 'carrying out death' that occurs at the end of Lent marking the end of winter. Lent was a period of time devoted to the needs of the spirit; it was a time of denial associated with certain austerities such as eating fish instead of meat. It was meant to remind Christians to distance themselves from earthly pleasures. Falstaff represents Carnival, Lord Flesh, and a time of indulgence where all the pleasures of the senses were entertained. The excesses associated with Carnival had to be relinquished during Lent. This was often dramatized as a battle between Carnival and Lent with Carnival represented by a fat man and Lent by an emaciated woman. At the end of Lent the defeated and enfeebled Carnival would be reduced to a skinny Jack-a-Lent and carried away in a ceremony celebrated as 'carrying out death'. It marked the Christian victory of the spiritual over the material.

In *The Merry Wives of Windsor* we see a similar victory when Falstaff is made small and insignificant by the superior wit of the wives. Falstaff, as in all his incarnations, is a creature of excess and the play delights in his 'waistfulness' and 'wantonness'. Yet despite allusions to this tradition no direct reference is made to it except when the Host, at one point, draws attention to the two warring forces (the material and the spiritual). He does so in a balanced conciliatory way respecting them both (concord in opposition); it is no battle that he encourages but rather a truce (3.1.91-96; 100)

Shall I lose my
doctor? No, he gives me the potions and the motions.
Shall I lose my parson? My priest? My Sir Hugh? No,
he gives me the proverbs and the no-verbs [to Caius]
Give me thy hand, terrestial; so. [to Evans] Give me
thy hand celestial; so. — Boys of art...
Follow me, lads of peace, follow, follow, follow.

So the tradition is there, in the background (the material versus the spiritual), but in this tale the wives are merry and not the emaciated hags of Lent nor the voluptuous seductresses of Carnival. They are the balance of virtuous moderation.

When Falstaff is finally exposed wearing horns he carries a richly multivalent symbolism attached to his person. Anne Parten points out that he is simultaneously the devil, the hunted deer, a fertility spirit, a scapegoat, a satyr, and Actaeon. Falstaff, like Carnival, is subject to change; he has his peaks and valleys and like Carnival he never goes away. Even at the end of the play he is exposed but not ostracized. He still has a place at the table.

c) The Host

The 'host of the Garter' is referred to by no other name than the 'Host'. There is something strangely biblical about this character. The play with its embedded history of Carnival and Lent, or more specifically with its discussion of the material and spiritual worlds, depicts the Host as its intercessor particularly in his role of peace maker between Dr. Caius and Pastor Evans. One cannot help but see allusions to Christ and of course to the host of the Eucharist (*Matthew* 26:26).

Jesus took bread, and blessed it, and brake it, and gave it to the disciples, and said, Take, eat; this is my body.

This is a play filled with translations and transformations; Falstaff is turned into a Windsor stag, the witch of Brainford, and a pile of dirty laundry so when we see the Host as the 'word made flesh' it is not particularly surprising. It should be noted that several words are also made into 'food' in the play. Parker points out some examples; Pastor Evans is presented as (5.5.142)

one that makes fritters of English.

He is also a man who translates *'Pauca verba'* as *'good worts'* (worts being words in his Welsh accent) which Falstaff further translates by turning *'worts'* into *'cabbage'* (1.1.120-121).

Evans is so dangerous with his mispronunciations that he strikes fear into Falstaff (5.5.81-82)

Heavens defend me from that Welsh fairy,
lest he transform me to a piece of cheese!

It could be Shakespeare was just indulging himself in word play but when we see the Germans (*three Doctor Faustuses*) take advantage of the Host and reduce him by stealing his horses (4.5.66) we cannot help but think of Luther, the German father of Protestantism, reducing the catholic host to a mere piece of bread. It is just one of many translations occurring in the play.

Just as Mistress Quickly embodies the spirit of Mercury as the messenger in the play the Host embodies the spirit of Christ as the major peace maker or go-between in the play by helping to resolve the majority of the disputes that arise between the characters. He embodies the very Christ-like role as intercessor.

d) Frank Ford

Ford, like Falstaff, is a character driven by his imagination. Ford's particular obsession is with being made into a cuckold. This combined with his innate jealousy makes him an extremely volatile character (2.1.89-90)

> *O, that my husband saw this letter!*
> *It would give eternal food to his jealousy.*

He is possessive of his property and that includes his wife. When he and Page are confronted by Pistol and Nim who reveal Falstaff's plan to seduce their wives (2.1.106)

> *Prevent, or go thou like Sir Actaeon he*

it is only Ford that believes in the scheme's possible success (2.2.168-169)

> *I do not misdoubt my wife, but I would be loath to*
> *turn them together. As man may be too confident.*

The seed of Falstaff's plan once planted in Ford's fertile imagination soon grows to the point that he actually subsidizes his own wife's seduction in order to confirm his worst fears of her.

Ford like all the other characters is translative. He changes himself into Brook and through the insanity of Brook he feeds his suspicions of his wife. Ford's obsession with being turned into a cuckold is demonstrated by his fear of being made to wear buck horns, the emblem of cuckoldry. This one thought consumes his mind and makes him *'horn mad'* (3.3.144-145)

> *Buck? I would I could wash myself of the buck!*
> *Buck, buck, buck! Ay buck!*

This madness grows until Ford is so insecure in his relationship that he associates marriage with infidelity (3.5.132-133)

> *This 'tis to be married, this 'tis to have linen and buck-*
> *baskets!*

Ford's meltdown occurs after Falstaff, hidden as dirty laundry in a buck-basket, is removed from the house for bucking (bleaching). Page and the others are aware of the gossip but Ford's public and unsuccessful search for his wife's lover is humiliating and they are shocked to see Ford air his own 'dirty laundry' so publicly (3.3.152-153)

> *Good Master Ford, be contented; you wrong*
> *yourself too much.*

Ford's obsession escalates. At the next appointed dalliance he beats a witch (the disguised Falstaff) from his home. Nancy Cotton sees the assault as a form of transference. He really wants to beat his wife. His frustration with the disconnect between her honesty and his suspicions erupts in an ironic tirade (4.2.121-123)

> *Mistress Ford, the*
> *honest woman, the modest wife, the virtuous creature*
> *that hath the jealous fool to her husband!*

His friends only see the truth in his ravings and view Ford as *'mad as a mad dog'* (4.2.118).

Cotton views Ford as a Page 'wannabe'. He is jealous of his friend. He is jealous of his confidence and his life. Ford has no children whereas Page has two, Anne and William. When Ford imagines his triumph over Falstaff he sees it as a triumph over the insufferable Page (2.2.291-295)

> *God be praised for*
> *my jealousy!...I will prevent*
> *this, detect my wife, be revenged on Falstaff and laugh*
> *at Page.*

Ford's statement climaxes with the expectation of revealing Page as a fool.

It is only after repeated failed attempts to show his wife as an adulteress and repeated humiliations of himself in front of his peers that Ford comes to his senses and learns the lesson of spousal trust. He asks his wife for forgiveness (4.4.6-8)

> *Pardon me, wife. Henceforth do what thou wilt:*
> *I rather will suspect the sun with cold*

> *Than thee with wantonness.*

With Ford's apology one senses that respect and trust has been restored in their marriage.

Ford's role is mainly to exaggerate Falstaff's; as Brook he adds flame to Falstaff's fire by subsidizing his seduction scheme and as Alice Ford's husband he pours cold water on these same seductions by interfering with their success. He both facilitates the amorous attacks and the churlish retreats. His actions 'embiggen' and make more credible the threat posed by Falstaff.

e) George Page

George Page is an aspiring middle class merchant, like Frank Ford, but he is a more balanced character. He trusts his wife and exercises no control over her. He does however wish to control who his daughter is to marry. He is a character wishing to advance his own status while at the same time hoping that traditional constraints control his daughter's place.

One of the most interesting features of Page is his name. Patricia Parker believes it to be part of the wordplay associated with the repeated allusions to Mercury (inventor of the written language and god of commerce) made in the play. Words being associated with the 'page' they are written on and the business of writing and publishing in general.

The play is filled with 'pages' in the form of letters, books, and print. Mistress Quickly acts as a 'page' in that she carries messages from one person to another. She performs a similar function to Falstaff's 'little page' Robin who initially delivers the multiple love letters to the wives. Multiple letters written on different pages is the 'brilliance' of Falstaff's plan and one of the reasons the women seek revenge (2.1.62-63; 66-70)

> *Letter for letter, but that the name of*
> *Page and Ford differs!*
> *I warrant he hath a thousand of these letters, writ*

> *with blank spaces for different names - sure, more, and these are of the second edition. He will print them, out of doubt; for he cares not what he puts into the press, when he would put us two.*

Shakespeare has drawn a poetic connection between the publishing industry and Falstaff's mass market plan of monetizing his sexuality with the literal name of Page.

f) The Wives and Daughter

It is the wives' interaction with Falstaff that creates the narrative of the play. It is a narrative loosely structured around three plays-within-the-play. These plays are the pranks directed, plotted, and staged by the wives to punish Falstaff for his acts of lechery and presumption. The 'prank-plays' are designed around three archetypal punishments for lust.

John Steadman links the 'basket episode' to a tale told about Virgil; it comes from *The Life of Virgil* and tells how a beautiful woman was pursued by Virgil and how she consented to meet with him at midnight if he climbed into a basket which would then be raised to her upper bed chamber window. Once 'basketed' he was raised halfway and left there till morning so that the people of Rome could laugh at his arrogance and wantonness.

Virgil's basket episode became well known as a symbol of love gone wrong or the evil effects of lust. In an image by Urs Graf (1519) Virgil is depicted as suspended in a basket while Cupid throws stones at him. In variants of the story the lover in the basket is dumped into a river or mud. These variants, Steadman presumes, were influenced by a German punishment for adulterers whereby they were dumped into a pool or mud puddle.

Falstaff's second punishment, his transformation into a woman, finds echoes in the story of Heracles' bondage to Omphale. It is a warning tale about the corrupting effects of lust and in it Heracles dresses and acts like a woman. The story is told in Ovid's *Heroides*.

The final playlet draws on both the mythological and iconological tradition for its symbolism. It is based on the tale of Actaeon and draws from Golding's translation of Ovid's *Metamorphoses*. The tale of Actaeon tells of a hunter who comes across naked Diana bathing. Diana, shocked at the effrontery of a mortal seeing her, turns him into a stag who is then chased and killed by his own dogs. Shakespeare substitutes being 'pinched' by fairies for being bitten by dogs but this is in keeping with Golding's translation since he too used the word 'pinch' for 'bite' when the dogs attacked Actaeon.

Ovid depicts Actaeon as an innocent victim of circumstances unjustly punished for being in the wrong place at the wrong time. But our Actaeon is neither innocent nor unaware of the when and where. Our Herne the Hunter, at the wives' bidding, transforms himself into a deer. This Circerean trick reveals to us that Falstaff is controlled by his senses and dominated by his animal nature. This is why the women publicly expose him; he is a rutting stag and as such a potential threat to all society. He is a would-be cuckolder that is 'outed' and outsmarted by the women he would victimize and so becomes a true cuckold himself (a victimized man).

The women do this virtuously without ever losing sight of the goal and employ means that are above reproach (2.1.87-89)

I will consent to act any villainy
against him, that may not sully the chariness of our
honesty.

The Actaeon story is an ambiguous one in that it suggests both the innocent victim as well as the rutting stag. He is in essence both the cuckold and the cuckolder. Actaeon, in Renaissance minds, became associated with the other tales of the punishment of lust because Actaeon's horns grew at the sight of naked Diana.

The wives not only direct the Actaeon drama involving Falstaff but they reveal themselves to be at the heart of a shifting power dynamic. The wives and to a lesser extent the daughter Anne demonstrate a way women can attain some degree of power in the community by avoiding official channels in favour of unofficial modes of social control.

These unofficial means constitute a form of tit for tat vengeance that is supported by the community so long as it is seen as just and appropriate (5.3.21-22)

> *Against such lewdsters and their lechery*
> *Those that betray them do no treachery.*

The wives reaffirm their own innocence by punishing Falstaff and anyone else who questions their honour. They are afforded the moral high ground. This virtuousness allows them to mete out punishments. Falstaff the deceiver who is deceived by the women shows himself and his plotting to be ineffective against their superior wit. Because of this Falstaff can be viewed as a cuckold, the symbol of the dominated man, and right subject of the skimmington presented. A skimmington had a particularly feminine flavour as often kitchen implements were employed as part of the punishment. People would bang on pots and pans with ladles as the victim was paraded around the town. Parten discusses the domesticity associated with the skimmington and Wall discusses fairylore employed in Falstaff's subsequent punishment. Together they show that Falstaff's punishments derive from this world of domestic females. The wives can be seen to extend their domestic power into the community by using what is available in their domain to isolate and punish the social threat posed by Falstaff. The wives, who spend much of the play repelling Falstaff's sexual advances, often describe him transformed into objects of housewifery. Falstaff is transformed/translated into *'gross fat pudding'* (2.1.26), whale oil (that could be used for candle wax) (2.1.57), and cooking grease (2.1.60); all manageable domestic goods.

Even Falstaff's Virgilesque punishment of being placed in a buck-basket was part of domestic duty. It involved bucking or bleaching dirty laundry. When Falstaff describes his confinement he does so by enlisting several other domestic duties such as distillation, making butter, and the making of stews (3.5.99-113).

The wives deal with Falstaff in the domestic realm and make their community the better for it thereby extending domestic control into the political realm and broadening their sphere of power.

Anne Page is yet another permutation on the theme of female power. Anne reflects the period's changing views concerning marriage. Marriages were traditionally arranged by the parents as a form of property transfer to an appropriate husband and often used to link or extend a family's fortunes. Anne's disobedience exercised against her parents' divergent wishes shows a culture where personal choice in marriage was gaining ground. It is a small power grab and not beyond the wishes of her parents (3.4.88-90)

> *I will not be your friend, nor enemy.*
> *My daughter will I question how she loves you,*
> *And as I find her, so am I affected*

but still reflects a broadening of the scope of women's power.

Conclusion

From the first initial reading of *The Merry Wives of Windsor* it is apparent that this is primarily a women's story about women's power and women's victory over a predatory man. It is a tale about a deceiver who is himself deceived by some very witty women. Inversion is a common enough technique used in a comedy but in this play it highlights the power wielded by middle class women over the men. The women, as a general statement, are the heroines in the piece and the men play ancillary roles, at best, or adversarial roles, at worst.

Falstaff hopes to commodify his sexuality by seducing the women and then exploiting their access to their families' wealth. He hopes to translate their wealth to himself. This, too, points out a major difference we see in the play. The men are primarily concerned over issues of money and property (material things) while the women are concerned with the more spiritual aspects of life like justice, honour, and love. The men's attention shows a preoccupation with wealth; Falstaff seeks access, via the wives, to the husbands' purses; Fenton, Slender, Caius all seek Anne Page's dowry; the Host has a tendency to overcharge or underserve his patrons and even Frank Ford's jealous concern over his wife is primarily a concern about property and its depreciation. The wives, on the other hand, show a concern with the community's well-being and their own honour. They see Falstaff as a threat to all women with his fill-in-the-blank seduction scheme and they hope, through the use of carefully staged acts of vengeance to both educate Frank Ford and remove the threat posed by Falstaff.

Translation is the central concept employed by Shakespeare to unify his play. It echoes throughout the comedy and its expanded meanings can be found everywhere. Translation is about taking, moving, interpreting, and changing. Translation is a many-faceted concept. At its heart is change (change in location, ownership or form) but it is also about understanding - one translates to reveal meaning. Translation implies a world of constant change, but it also implies a world of revealed meaning. It is an active verb characterizing an active society, a society where everything changes and nothing is static. It is a society where actions must be interpreted to be understood but not presumed to be based on a static and past tradition. This of course is the essence of the

Garter Motto *"Honi soit qui mal y pense"*, Shame on him who thinks evil of it, (i.e.) presumption, assuming you know, is at the core of its warning. Falstaff sees an opportunity in the wives' merriment and hopes to exploit their presumed lust. Ford, too, presumes his wife is unfaithful and as his translated self, Brook, subsidizes Falstaff's efforts at her seduction and his affirmation. These men make assumptions. They translate a behavior - being merry - into morality. They believe the women are loose. It is a presumption for which the men are punished.

The middle class society of the play is one of change. Power is no longer irrefutably linked to inheritance and an established hierarchy but now appears to be a purchasable commodity. This is a capitalist society where 'money goes before'. Money is the new means to access power. The traditional understanding of privilege and the power that accompanies it are being called into question. Falstaff, a knight of the old order, a member of the upper class, has fallen on hard times and is now being called into account for his scandalous behaviour. Society is transforming, translating itself into something new. Money is the scorecard used by this emerging meritocracy, worth being measured by one's ability to accumulate and distribute wealth. This reflects a more democratic form of power than inherited wealth or title in that it is expansive and more inclusive for it rewards those gifted enough to seize an opportunity. These aspects of wealth and property form a subtext that informs the drama but it is a concern mainly of the males - Falstaff, Fenton, Ford, et.al. - it acts as the fuel to their actions but does little to explain the actions of the women.

What the women are interested in is control. They initially wish to defend their honour but expand their goals for the protection of the community. Society is changing and so is the place of women in it. Alice Ford is seen by her husband Frank as a possession but he soon learns she is an independent 'sun' worthy of his trust and love. The women operate outside the formal systems set up by the males (courts, churches) and their justice depends on the community and its standards. They constitute a form of social justice exercised publicly and transparently through processes such as a skimmington.

In the end it is the women that defend their honour and their right to act freely - to choose to laugh and be merry. Human rights, like the right to choose a husband, appear to be in the domain of the women. Independence of purpose, self-determination, is the fuel that drives the women. The new form of marriage that is presented is a partnership and not the purchase or translation of chattel from parent to husband.

The play itself, or more specifically the Windsor community, appears to be organized around concepts central to the god Mercury. Mercury/Hermes was the god associated with language, trade and commerce, as well as with theft and cunning. Mercury was the leader of the three Graces. The Graces embodied the idea of 'harmony in discord' or 'passion and restraint'. They were the productive triad (passion, chastity, and beauty) that symbolized ordered change from the innocence of chastity through passion to the beauty of fulfilled love (a Ficinian idea drawn from the Orphic mysteries). In himself, Mercury is a balanced figure and reflects a balanced society productive but with an undercurrent of the avarice needed for motivation. Pistol, Nim, and Bardolph are thieves and con men but they do not require explicit action taken against them. It is Falstaff that crosses the boundary, it is he that goes beyond the pale; even Pistol and Nim do not support his actions.

Falstaff is a manifestation of yet another god, Bacchus/Dionysis, the sensual god of chaos and disorder. Lord Flesh threatens the order of this mercurial society with disorder. Falstaff is no respecter of authority or boundaries. He is the force of anarchy and misrule that can destroy a society. He is pure sensual greed; excess without limit. The wives contain and expose him; they limit his ability to act and bring harmony (ordered change) back into the community.

Falstaff's disruptive presence is not without some good. He exposes Ford's excessive possessiveness over his wife and his humiliation as 'Herne the hunter' provides the distraction necessary for Anne Page to elope with Fenton in a love match of her own choosing.

The play is about change - ordered, virtuous change. It reflects changing societies, changing language, and changing traditions. It is not without note that the villain in the piece is Falstaff, the most English of the characters; a member of the traditional upper class. In a play filled with foreigners it is Falstaff, a representative of English tradition, who is the biggest threat to the society. It is he that marginalizes, underestimates and stereotypes the women and it is he that hopes to take advantage of and steal from the growing middle class.

Bibliography

1) *The Merry Wives of Windsor*, William Shakespeare, edited by Giorgio Melchiori, The Arden Shakespeare, Third Series, Cengage Learning, 2000.
2) *Shakespeare from the Margins: Language, Culture, Context*, Patricia Parker, Chapter 1, Preposterous Events: From Late to Early Shakespeare, p. 20-55; Chapter 4, "Illegitimate Construction": Translation, Adultery, and Mechanical Reproduction in *The Merry Wives of Windsor*, p. 116-148, The University of Chicago Press, 1996.
3) *The "ill kill'd" Deer: Poaching and Social Order in 'The Merry Wives of Windsor'*, Jeffrey Theis, *Texas Studies in Literature and Language*, Vol. 43, No. 1, Renaissance Review: Wyatt, Spenser, Shakespeare, and Heywood (Spring, 2001), p.46-73.
4) *Castrating (W)itches: Impotence and Magic in 'The Merry Wives of Windsor'*, Nancy Cotton, *Shakespeare Quarterly*, Vol. 38, No. 3 (Autumn, 1987), p.320-326.
5) *Falstaff's Horns: Masculine Inadequacy and Feminine Mirth in 'The Merry Wives of Windsor'*, Anne Parten, *Studies in Philology*, Vol. 82, No. 2 (Spring, 1985), p.184-199.
6) *Falstaff in Windsor Forest: Villain or Victim?*, Jeanne Addison Roberts, *Shakespeare Quarterly*, Vol. 26, No. 1 (Winter, 1975), p.8-15.
7) *Why Does Puck Sweep? Fairylore, Merry Wives, and Social Struggle*, Wendy Wall, *Shakespeare Quarterly*, Vol. 52, No. 1 (Spring, 2001), p.67-106.
8) *Falstaff as Actaeon: A Dramatic Emblem*, John M. Steadman, *Shakespeare Quarterly*, Vol. 14, No. 3 (Summer, 1963), p.231-244.

9) *"A Received Belief": Imagination in 'The Merry Wives of Windsor'*, William Carroll, *Studies in Philology*, Vol.74, No.2 (April, 1977), p.186-215.

10) *The Meaning of Falstaff's Allusion to the Jack-a-Lent in 'The Merry Wives of Windsor'*, Frederick B. Jonassen, *Studies in Philology*, Vol. 88, No. 1 (Winter, 1991), p.46-68.

11) *"I am made an ass": Falstaff and the Scatology of Windsor's Polity*, Will Stockton, *Texas Studies in Literature and Language*, Vol. 49, No. 4 (Winter, 2007), p.340-360.

12) *Shakespearean Chronology, Ideological Complicity, and Floating Texts: Something is Rotten in Windsor*, Barbara Freedman, *Shakespeare Quarterly*, Vol. 45, No. 2 (Summer, 1994), p.190-210.

13) *Doctor Faustus and 'The Merry Wives of Windsor'*, Robert A.H. Smith, *The Review of English Studies*, New Series, Vol. 43, No. 171 (August, 1992), p.395-397.

14) *New Larousse Encyclopedia of Mythology*, translated by Richard Aldington and Delano Ames, edited by Felix Guirand, Hamlyn Publishing Group, 1982, p. 123-124.

15) *Pagan Mysteries in the Renaissance*, Edgar Wind, W.W. Norton and Co. Inc., 1968, p. 113-127.

Coriolanus: The Making of Monsters

Introduction

Rigid pride is often cited as Coriolanus's failing. I intend to dispel this myth by demonstrating that Coriolanus is instead an example of Aristotle's Great-Souled man and that the tale told of Rome's disintegration is the direct result of its creation of two monsters: one that acts from without and the other from within. These monsters are the manifestations of another of Aristotle's principles; namely, the dialectic that he felt existed between confidence and fear. When these qualities exist in individuals in their extreme forms (excess confidence as displayed in Coriolanus and excessive fear as manifest by the public) they create personality types that are capable of fragmenting the cohesiveness of Rome and undermining the nature of community. It is Coriolanus's sense of honour and his confidence in his moral position that undermines Rome by striking fear into an abused populous that is controlled by an equally fearful group of senators.

Plutarch's *Lives* or more specifically North's English translation of J. Amyot's French version of Plutarch's Greek text *The Lives of the Nobel Grecians and Romans* provides the source material for *Coriolanus* (written 1605-1610). Sharing this same source material and written at approximately the same time was another of Shakespeare's plays, *Timon of Athens*. Plutarch in his *Lives* sets up a series of comparable biographies, parallel lives, between Greeks and their Roman counterparts; Coriolanus (Roman) and Alcibiades (Greek) are one such pair. Shakespeare employed Alcibiades' biography in *Timon of Athens* and his Roman counterpart in *Coriolanus*. The characters are 'peas in a pod' for both are examples of what Aristotle referred to as the 'Great-souled man' (see *Presence in Absence*, S.W. Stout, The Mean Spirit in Timon, p. 11-14). Many critics believe that Coriolanus suffers from an excess of pride (*Coriolanus*, The Arden Shakespeare, edited by Philip Brockbank, Introduction, p.37)

"Pride is the essence of Martius' nature, at once his vice and his virtue".

I intend to show this is not the case by revealing Martius Coriolanus's true nature is that of the Great-Souled man and that his tragedy is not the result of his pride but rather is due to the hubris of the Roman people.

The Great-Souled Man

"Therefore the great-souled man is he who has the right disposition in relation to honours and disgraces...honour is the object with which the great-souled are concerned, since it is honour above all else which great men claim and deserve."

(Aristotle, *Nicomachean Ethics*, IV.iii.10-11)

The 'Great-Souled Man' is a personality type that Aristotle defined in his Nicomachean Ethics. It is a virtuous, though not always appealing, personality that can appear to be proud but is not so undeservedly. The Great-souled are as close to god-like as humans can get. They are of exceptional ability and are deserving of all the superlatives applied to them. Because of their physical and moral superiority they often are perceived as aloof and judgmental of the world around them. Martius Coriolanus is not proud but rather is great-souled. To demonstrate this I will alternately quote from Aristotle's Nicomachean Ethics and then from Shakespeare's Coriolanus in order to show the parallels that exist between the two. Aristotle's Nicomachean Ethics existed in English translation as early as 1547 and his *Politics* was available by 1598. In Shakespeare's poetry we find an amalgamating of Aristotelian ideas with the Plutarchian plot points producing a fluid mix that is superior to both.

Aristotle believed the great-souled manifested the awful virtues of discipline, hard work and sacrifice and therefore deserved (but would never ask for) honour
(*Nicomachean Ethics* IV.iii.3)

"*Now a person is thought to be great-souled if he claims much and deserves much*".

(2.1.136-138)

> Vol.: *In troth, there's wondrous things spoke of him.*
> Men.: *Wondrous! Ay, I warrant you, and not without*
> *His true purchasing.*

The great-souled serve a higher ideal so like a priest or a zealot have little concern for worldly comforts (*Nicomachean Ethics* IV.iii.18)

"*The great-souled man...will not rejoice overmuch in prosperity, nor grieve overmuch at adversity...he therefore to whom even honour is a small thing will be indifferent to other things as well. Hence great-souled men are thought to be haughty*".

(3.2.124-128)

> *Our spoils he kick'd at,*
> *And looked upon things precious as they were*
> *The common muck of the world. He covets less*
> *Than misery itself would give, rewards*
> *His deeds with doing them.*

The great-souled cannot be fooled or manipulated with praise (*Nicomachean Ethics* IV.iii.30)

"*He is not prone to admiration, since nothing is great to him*".

(1.9.13-17)

> *My mother,*
> *Who has a charter to extol her blood,*
> *When she does praise me, grieves me. I have done*
> *As I have done, that's what I can; induc'd*

> *As you have been, that's for my country.*

also (1.9.28-29)

> *I have some wounds upon me, and they smart*
> *To hear themselves remember'd.*

The great-souled will face danger nobly for a noble cause and war is considered a noble cause (*Nicomachean Ethics* IV.iii.23)

> *"The great-souled man does not run into danger for trifling reasons, and is not a lover of danger...but he will face danger in a great cause".*

(1.4.53)

> *Oh noble fellow!*
> *Who sensibly outdares his senseless sword.*

The great-souled will not shirk their duty and will also help others with theirs (*Nicomachean Ethics* IV.iii.26)

> *"It is also characteristic of the great-souled man never to ask help from others, or only with reluctance but to render aid willingly".*

(1.4.10-12)

> *Now Mars, I prithee make us quick in work,*
> *That we with smoking swords may march from hence*
> *To help our fielded friends.*

Coriolanus also leads by example (1.4.45)

> *Mark me, and do the like!*

The great-souled man has many traits that are easy to admire but he was also considered to be morally superior to others so could be arrogant and judgmental in his relationships because of this same moral insight (*Nicomachean Ethics* IV.iii.22)

> *"For the great-souled man is justified in despising other people – his estimates are correct".*

Because the great-souled man was considered to be truthful and just his just judgments were considered to be accurate but rarely flattering. So when Coriolanus condemns his troops as cowards it is because they are. (1.4.34-36)

> *You souls of geese,*
> *That bear the shapes of men, how have you run*
> *From slaves that apes would beat!*

He is even unkind but equally accurate in his assessment of the citizens of Rome (1.1.169-173; 176-181)

> *He that trusts to you.*
> *Where he should find you lions, finds you hares;*
> *Where foxes, geese: you are no surer, no,*
> *Than is the coal of fire upon the ice,*
> *Or hailstones in the sun.*
> *...your affections are*
> *A sick man's appetite, who desires most that*
> *Which would increase his evil. He that depends*
> *Upon your favours, swims with fins of lead.*
> *...Hang ye! Trust ye?*
> *With every minute you do change a mind.*

Coriolanus is not a sympathetic character but he is open. What you see is what you get. He does not deceive and it is this very trait that allows his enemies to manipulate him. This lack of guile is a characteristic of the great-souled man (*Nicomachean Ethics* IV.iii.28)

"He must be open both in love and in hate, since concealment show timidity; and care more for the truth than for what people think".

In Shakespeare's play Menenius describes Coriolanus (3.1.253-256)

> *His nature is too noble for the world:*
> *He would not flatter Neptune for his trident,*
> *Or Jove for's power to thunder. His heart's his mouth:*

> *What his breast forges, that his tongue must vent.*

Menenius tries to curb his openness by reminding Coriolanus (3.1.238)

> *Put not your worthy rage into your tongue.*

His honesty goads the people (3.1.124;121)

> *Did not deserve corn gratis*
> *They ne'er did service for't*

but he is equally frank with the Senators who he considers weak and indulgent (3.1.91; 97-101)

> *You grave but reckless senators...awake*
> *Your dangerous lenity. If you are learn'd*
> *Be not as common fools; if you are not*
> *Let them have cushions by you. You are plebians*
> *If they be senators.*

His honesty cannot be curbed and despite Volumnia's maternal advice to dissemble (3.2.52-57) and her instruction *"Go, and be rul'd"* (3.2.90) he cannot acquiesce. Aristotle speaks to this point (Nicomachean Ethics IV.iii.29)

> *"He will be incapable of living at the will of another...since to do so is slavish".*

Martius Coriolanus is defined by honour, in that he tries to act honourably and in honourable circumstances, by so doing he achieves honour and fame but these are side benefits and not his intended goals (*Nicomachean Ethics* IV.iii.23)

> *"The great-souled man...will face danger in a great cause, and when so doing will be ready to sacrifice his life, since he holds that life is not worth having at every price".*

(1.6.71-72; 74-75)

> *If any think brave death outweighs bad life,*
> *And that his country's dearer than himself;*
> *Wave thus to express his disposition,*

And follow Martius.

One other incident of weakness in Coriolanus actually supports this claim that he is a great-souled man. The incident involves his forgetting a name (1.9.80-84; 85; 88)

> Cor.: *I sometime lay here in Corioles,*
> *At a poor man's house: he us'd me kindly.*
> *He cried to me. I saw him prisoner.*
> *...I request you*
> *To give my poor host freedom.*
> Com.: *Oh well begg'd!*
> Lar.: *Martius, his name?*
> Cor.: *By Jupiter, forgot!*

According to Aristotle (*Nicomachean Ethics* IV.iii.24; 25) the great-souled man

"is fond of conferring benefits, but ashamed to receive them, because the former is a mark of superiority and the latter inferiority"

therefore

"The great-souled are thought to have a good memory for any benefit they have conferred, but a bad memory for those which they have received".

I believe from such arguments it is clear that Martius Coriolanus qualifies as a great-souled man. He is, however, not perfect but his imperfection lies not in pride but in rashness. Again we will use Aristotle as our source to understand not only Coriolanus's weakness but also those of Aufidius, Volumnia, and the Roman people.

The Rash Man

"The observance of the mean in fear and confidence is courage...he that exceeds in confidence is Rash; he that exceeds in fear and is deficient in confidence is Cowardly" (*Nicomachean Ethics* II.vii.2)

Cominius purports that courage (valour/fortitude) is the chief virtue (2.2.84-85)

That valour is the chiefest virtue and
Most dignifies the haver.

Courage (valour) along with Prudence (practical wisdom), Temperance (moderation), and Justice (equanimity, truth, correctness) make up the four virtues. Aristotle discusses them in his *Nicomachean Ethics* but he concludes that (*Nicomachean Ethics* V.i.15)

"Justice...is perfect Virtue...it is displayed towards others. This is why Justice is often thought to be the chief of the Virtues...

When Cominius singles out courage (valour) as the chief virtue he is making an ethical error and perhaps celebrating one of the virtues to excess. We know from Aristotle that when confidence exceeds the mean point of courage it manifests itself as rashness (behaviour that is reckless, foolhardy, impulsive or hastily conceived). In Rome we have a society that celebrates courage as the primary virtue; they value it to the point of excess, so it should come as no surprise that Coriolanus could exceed the norm in his pursuit of his country's most valued virtue and become rash in the process.

The rash man performs actions with little thought of the consequences and often on the spur of the moment. The storming of the gates of Corioli is one such example, although it could be argued that timing was of the essence. The Volsces were fleeing to their city's open gates and Martius felt his troops would support his actions in taking advantage of this opportunity. Nevertheless his decision was hasty and could probably be seen as rash (1.4.42-45)

...Follow me!
So, now the gates are ope. Now prove good seconds!
'Tis for the followers Fortune widens them,

> *Not for the fliers. Mark me, and do the like!*

It is Coriolanus's impulsiveness that seems to win over any considered judgment (1.9.83)

> *...wrath o'whelm'd my pity.*

Even his fellow Senators cannot control his impulsiveness. Granted we know the great-souled are *"incapable of living at the will of another"* but still his actions exceed what is in his own best interests. It is this recklessness with his future that gives credence to the charge of rashness. For example when Brutus and Sicinius incense the people against him (3.1.30) he does not walk away but rather chooses to make matters worse (3.1.57; 60-63; 74)

> Men.: *Let's be calm.*
> Cor.: *Tell me of corn!*
> *This was my speech, and I will speak't again.*
> Men.: *Not now, not now.*
> Sen.: *Not in this heat, sir, now.*
> Cor.: *Now as I live, I will...*
> Sen.: *No more words, we beseech you.*

His righteous contempt for the citizens of Rome and his considered opinion of how the Senate is indulging the people (essentially fueling a democratic rebellion and their own demise) are opinions not without merit; Coriolanus truly believes that he knows what's best for the people of Rome and her Senators. The confidence he displays in his conclusions are typical of the great-souled man that he is, but his inability to curb his own tongue and his inability to restrain himself from voicing these opinions before a hostile audience show a singular lack of judgment and a recklessness on his part.

This self destructive behaviour is repeated later on with both Menenius and his mother, Volumnia, trying to talk sense into him. Volumnia points out that he has in essence passed the mean-point of courage in the dialectic between confidence and fear and that by exceeding the mean he has in fact diminished himself (3.2.19-20)

> *You might have been enough the man you are,*
> *With striving less to be so.*

She councils consideration (3.2.29-31)

> *I have a heart as little apt as yours*
> *But yet a brain that leads my use of anger*
> *To better vantage.*

She warns him of his own extremity, a type of fundamentalist excess that will not be curbed or be respectful of others (3.2.39; 41-43)

> *You are too absolute.*
> *I have heard you say,*
> *Honour and policy, like unsever'd friends,*
> *I'th'war do grow together.*

She hopes he will act with policy (statecraft, shrewdness, prudence). Cominius also coaches Coriolanus to act mildly (3.2.138-139)

> *...arm yourself*
> *To answer mildly.*

The word is then repeated four more times as the conversation continues (3.2.142-145)

> Cor.: *The word is 'mildly'...*
> Men.: *Ay, but mildly.*
> Cor.: *Well, mildly be it then. Mildly!*

Although Coriolanus promises 'mildness' timidity is not in his nature nor is subterfuge. He is quickly goaded by the tribunes into speaking his mind (3.3.27-29)

> *Put him to choler straight...*
> *Being once chaf'd, he cannot*
> *Be rein'd again to temperance; then he speaks*
> *What's in his heart.*

They do this by calling him a traitor (impugning his honour) and charging him with treason (3.3.63-66)

> *We charge you, that you have contriv'd to take*
> *From Rome all season'd* (established) *office, and to wind*
> *Yourself into a power tyrannical;*
> *For which you are a traitor to the people.*

Coriolanus does not calm the audience nor does he reassure them that he has no intention of limiting their power, rather he engages the tribunes as he would an enemy by using invectives and verbal assaults. Despite his awareness that he was going into a charged situation and the promises he made to behave mildly he cannot curb his nature and his rash responses (3.3.120-123; 90-91)

> *You common cry of curs! Whose breath I hate*
> *As the reek o'th' rotten fens, whose love I prize*
> *As the dead carcasses of unburied men*
> *That do corrupt my air*
> *I would not buy*
> (Your) *mercy at the price of one fair word.*

Coriolanus's outburst combined with a hand-picked crowd of dissenters leads to his banishment from Rome but not from impetuous behavior. Coriolanus is a constant character willing to bear the cost of who he is. He reassures his mother of his unchangeable nature (4.1.51-53)

> *While I remain above the ground you shall*
> *Hear from me still, and never of me aught*
> *But what is like me formerly.*

Unfortunately to be unchangeable is to be predictable and hence exploitable. Aufidius is well aware of Coriolanus's behavior (4.7.35-47) and uses him for his military skill and commitment to purpose. Once done he disposes of him in the exact same manner as did the tribunes before. He exploits his volatile nature by calling his honour into question. He too accuses him of being a traitor (5.4.85-86)

But tell the traitor in the highest degree
He hath abus'd your powers.

Aufidius lies about the peace achieved and his role in it; he accuses Coriolanus of *"Breaking his oath"* and *"never admitting Counsel o'th'war"* in the drawing up of the treaty with Rome. Yet we know Coriolanus did nothing in private (5.3.92-93)

Aufidius, and you Volsces, mark; for we'll
Hear nought from Rome in private

and we also know that Aufidius was responsible for the peace agreement (5.3.196-198)

But, good sir, (Aufidius)
What peace you'll make, advise me. For my part,
I'll not to Rome, I'll back with you.

Coriolanus can defend his statements (5.6.71-84) made to the Consuls and dismiss Aufidius's accusations but he sees Aufidius's attack as personal and looks only to himself for defense; reason is cast aside and his rash response directed at Aufidius inflames the wider audience (5.6.120)

Tear him to pieces! Do it presently!

Even the consuls see Coriolanus's ill considered response as contributory to his own death (5.6.144-145)

His own impatience
Takes from Aufidius a great part of blame.

Confidence is the ability to cope with any situation on your own, it is an expression of self-reliance. Coriolanus exceeds in confidence to the point where he is certain he can cope with any situation, even banishment; this makes him uncontrollable and rash for he is reliant on nobody for anything. He is an independent operator. He is the antithesis of the urban man. Unfortunately this leads him into impossible situations, situations he could easily avoid by using the minimum of discretion. This is his fatal flaw, when he is pushed he only ever chooses to push back.

The Fearful Man

The extreme points of Aristotle's dynamic are Rashness and Cowardice. Rashness arises from extreme confidence and Cowardice arises from fear and a lack of confidence. Fear is the adjective most applied to the plebeians and they are the extreme opposite to Coriolanus.

A city arises from a collective fear. People recognize their vulnerability as individuals and choose to live in groups. What they lack in courage or strength can be compensated for by larger numbers. This mutual need for safety requires individuals to recognize that they are not self-sufficient and to voluntarily surrender some of their autonomy and freedoms in order to share in the communal life and protection that a city offers. It is a form of risk management.

What is the city but the people? (3.1.197)

When the play begins the people (the mob, the plebs) plan a rebellion for they are in fear of starvation (1.1.3-4)

You are all resolved rather to die than to Famish?

They fear they are disposable and, in Coriolanus's eyes, they are (1.1.223-225)

Mess.: *The Volsces are in arms.*

Mar.: *I am glad on't; then we shall ha'means to vent Our musty superfluity.*

Martius Coriolanus means to press into service those individuals who are mutinous and seditious thereby removing the unruly element from Rome as well as alleviating some of the overcrowding. The populace are aware of this type of behavior by the patrician ruling class and justifiably fear both famine and the patricians' control over them.

Martius sees the common people and the troops drawn from these commoners (the rank and file) as untrustworthy cowards (1.6.43-44)

> *The common file – a plague!*
> *The mouse ne'er shunn'd the cat as they did budge*
> *from rascals worse than they*

and (1.1.170-171)

> *Where he should find you lions, finds you hares;*
> *Where foxes, geese.*

The plebs are not self-sufficient, they do not control their own circumstances. They are dependent on the senators for fixing food prices, the cost of borrowing and for establishing the laws that govern the city (1.1.78-84)

> *Care for us? True indeed! They ne'er cared*
> *for us yet. Suffer us to famish, and their store-*
> *houses crammed with grain; make edicts for usury,*
> *to support usurers; repeal daily any wholesome act*
> *established against the rich, and provide more*
> *piercing statutes daily, to chain up and restrain the*
> *poor. If the wars eat us not up, they will.*

They are equally dependent on the military, soldiers like Coriolanus, who guard and protect the city. To be dependent puts them in a dangerous position where they lack control over the very circumstances that affect their lives. In the end they fear what they cannot control.

It is not just the people that are fearful of the senators and consuls but so are the tribunes (whom the people elected). These tribunes fear for their jobs and a loss of power should Coriolanus be named a new consul (2.1.219-221)

> Sic.: *On the sudden, I warrant him consul.*

Bru.: *Then our office may,*

> *During his power, go sleep.*

The tribunes, acting out of their own fears, then exploit the people's general fears by manipulating them to act against Coriolanus and recall their approval of his consulship (2.1.243-250)

> *We must suggest* (remind) *the people in what hatred*
> *He still hath held them: that to's power he would*
> *Have made them mules, silenc'd their pleaders, and*
> *Dispropertied* (dispossessed) *their freedoms; holding them,*
> *In human action and capacity,*
> *Of no more soul nor fitness for the world*
> *Than camels in their war, who have their provand* (food)
> *Only for bearing burthens.*

They play on the people's fear of a dark possible future and their lack of trust in an aloof and unapproachable Coriolanus, a figure so distant from the people as courage is from cowardice. To them he is a 'thing removed' more than a fellow citizen.

The tribunes also perceive Coriolanus as something other than human and less sympathetic (3.1.79-81)

> *You speak o'th'people*
> *As if you were a god to punish, not*
> *A man of their infirmity.*

More often than not Coriolanus is described as a thing (2.2.108-110)

> *...from face to foot*
> *He was a thing of blood, whose every motion*
> *Was tim'd with dying cries*

and not just a thing but a thing to fear (5.4.12-14; 18-24)

> *This Martius is*
> *grown from man to dragon: he has wings: he's more*
> *than a creeping thing.*

When he walks, he
moves like an engine and the ground shrinks before
his trending. He is able to pierce a corslet with his
eye, talks like a knell, and his hum is a battery. He
sits in his state as a thing made for Alexander.
What he bids be done is finished with his bidding.
He wants nothing of a god but eternity.

It is the fear the people harbor towards him that leads to his exile. Aufidius speaks of this in his synopsis of Coriolanus's nature (4.7.35-48)

Whether 'twas pride...
whether defect of judgment...
or whether nature,
Not to be other than one thing...but commanding peace
As he controll'd the war; but one of these –
...made him fear'd,
So hated, and so banish'd.

The people cannot relate to Coriolanus. He is not *'a man of their infirmity'*. It is not enough that the other Generals testify for him or that the soldiers tell tales of him. The people have to touch his celebrity to know he's human. This is why the marketplace scene is so important. They need to see his wounds to know he can be hurt, to know he suffers as they do, to know he is fragile. The scene is about the people trying to glimpse the human, mortal part of Coriolanus.

People Hate Those Things They Fear

Coriolanus has isolated himself from everyone; patricians and plebs alike. This is not just a result of his independence and self-reliance but seems to be a property intrinsic to himself. He is possessed with an otherness the makes him different from his fellow citizens.

F.N. Lees described Coriolanus as a man with great martial gifts but who is crippled by a pitiful lack of human feeling to the point that he is unfitted for life as a social being; Coriolanus, he feels, has an 'undeveloped heart'. This is not all that surprising since he grew up in the wars (1.1.5-6; 14)

> *When yet he was*
> *But tender-bodied...*
> *To a cruel war I sent him*

also (3.1.317-318)

> *...he has been bred i'th'wars*
> *Since a could draw a sword.*

Empathy is not an asset during war and sadly the ability to dehumanize the enemy also helps one to cope. Combined, these disabilities make Coriolanus what he is: machine-like, insentient, and inhuman. Throughout the play Coriolanus is seen as something other than human and, perhaps more frightening, he is seen as something that can't be controlled.

Coriolanus is spoken of as a god at least seven times in the play (2.1.217), (2.1.264), (3.1.79-81), (4.6.91-96), (5.3.11), (5.3.34-36), and (5.4.24). He is also spoken of as a beast at least as many times. He is called *"a very dog"* (1.1.27), *"a steed"* (1.9.12), *"a lamb, a bear"* (2.1.10), *"a viper"* (3.1.261), *"a dragon"* (5.9.13), and *"a male tiger"* (5.9.29). Because of this conjunction of god and animal imagery Lees believes we are purposefully reminded of the phrase from Aristotle's *Politics* (Book 1, 1253a)

> *"He that is incapable of living in a society is a god or a beast."*

Coriolanus is both, and therefore ill-suited to city life. He stirs up dissention wherever he goes (2.2.18-19)

> *But he seeks their hate with*
> *greater devotion than they can render it him*

whether it be insulting the plebs for lack of service or reprimanding the Senators for their leniency (3.1.65-71)

> *For the mutable, rank-scented meinie, let them*
> *Regard me as I do not flatter, and*
> *Therein behold themselves. I say again,*
> *In soothing them, we nourish 'gainst our senate*
> *The cockle of rebellion, insolence sedition,*
> *Which we ourselves have plough'd for, sow'd and scatter'd,*
> *By mingling them with us.*

His gifts and his aloofness create the impression that he is something other, something removed; an impression that finds expression throughout the play. He fancies himself, like the gods, to be self-created. He earns his own name through his actions (1.9.62; 64)

> *For what he did before Corioles, call him*
> *Martius Caius Coriolanus!*

He purposefully severs the human bond with family (5.3.34-36)

> *I'll never*
> *Be such a gosling to obey instinct, but stand*
> *As if a man were author of himself*
> *And knew no other kin.*

Through his feats and leadership he creates the impression that he is immortal (4.6.91-96)

> *He is their god. He leads them like a thing*
> *Made by some other deity than nature,*
> *That shapes man better; and they follow him*
> *...with no less confidence*
> *Than boys pursing summer butterflies,*
> *Or butchers killing flies.*

This idea that Coriolanus is not human, perhaps even fatal to human life, is a theme that runs through the play (2.1.159-160)

> *Death, that dark spirit, in's nervy arm doth lie,*
> *Which, being advanc'd, declines, and then men die*

or (2.2.107-108)

> *...his sword, death's stamp,*
> *Where it did mark, it took.*

Coriolanus is a thing that seems to be uncontrollable by the society that created him. This creates a sense of societal paranoia that the play shares with other ancient tales such as that of the Golem from Jewish mysticism. Shakespeare was aware of Jewish mystical texts as can be seen from his inclusion of ideas from the Kabbalah in his work *The Merchant of Venice* (1598) (*In Sheep's Clothing*, S.W. Stout, The Character of Cabala, p. 64-83). Whether he had any direct exposure to the tale of the Golem is uncertain but the story does offer us certain insights to better understand the drama in *Coriolanus*.

The story of the Golem involves a rabbi who uses his esoteric knowledge of how God created Adam to mimic the process and create his own servant, a golem, from clay. The golem was generally created in a time of danger to defend the Jewish people but at some point the golem becomes uncontrollable and a threat to those whom it was intended to serve. In some stories the word 'emet' (truth) was written on the forehead of the 'molded formed clay mass' to bring it to life. The golem could then be deactivated by removing the aleph from 'emet' changing the word to 'met' and changing its meaning from 'truth' to 'death'.

In *Coriolanus* we encounter some similar ideas. A soldier of exceptional ability is created by a determined mother *"the honour'd mould/Wherein this trunk was framed"* (5.3.22-23) and raised in the crucible of war to serve the Roman people. This soldier speaks and acts truthfully but he is feared by the people as something other than human, a type of monster that they cannot relate to. Their refusal to honour him and inability to control him eventually leads to his exile and his decision to take revenge against his ungrateful city.

It is a tale of 'hubris' but it is not the 'monster's pride' that is out of control but rather the pride of those that used the monster and failed to justly honour or respect the life they created (2.3.9-10)

> *Ingratitude*
> *is monstrous, and for the multitude to be*
> *ingrateful, were to make a monster of the multitude.*

It is hubris to demand a service and then to choose not to confer a benefit for that service. It is common sense to realize that everything has a cost. This is how we plan for and prepare for the consequences of our actions. When we demand a service but are not willing to pay for that service it reveals in us a sense of entitlement or the belief that somehow we are deserving of benefits 'gratis'.

The people (including Senators) of Rome suffer from hubris. When they realize Coriolanus is going to exact revenge for his humiliation they become aware of the cost of their ingratitude (5.4.31-35)

> Sic.: *The gods be good unto us.*
> Men.: *No, in such case the gods will not be good unto*
> *us. When we banished him, we respected not them;*
> *and, he returning to break our necks, they respect*
> *not us.*

It is the people's fear of Coriolanus that clouds their judgment and creates the emotional distance between them. They do not see him as one of them and he is, in effect, isolated from them even as he lives among them. Their fear can be attributed to or generalized as a fear of the exceptional, or the different, or even the new and it is this popular fear that places *Coriolanus* in the same lineage as Shelly's *Frankenstein* (1818), or Philip Dick's cautionary tales of robots; all these presaging the

Terminator movies wherein the creation sets about to destroy the world of their human creators.

Coriolanus is a tool of destruction, a thing of death; he does not easily fit in with the social fabric of the city. This force of 'anti-life' has been raised with humans but it is through his least social features that he has managed to rise above them to become something else (5.4.12-14)

This Martius is

grown from man to dragon: he has wings: he's more

than a creeping thing.

Coriolanus's presence is tolerated and at times celebrated because he performs a useful function but he lacks the skills, training, and moral flexibility to navigate the social world. He is incapable of compromise and so represents a problem to a morally grey society. Because he is a warrior and lacks social empathy his decisions, if given political power, could put citizens in harm's way. He has, on more than one occasion, indicated that he would allow the city to be destroyed before he would compromise his values; for example, when the citizens were given tribunes to represent their grievances before the senate Coriolanus responded that he would have never granted such a request (1.1.216-218)

's death,

The rabble should have first unroof'd the city

Ere so prevail' with me.

Without an inherent empathy or friendliness towards humanity Coriolanus could easily make decisions that are deemed psychotic and potentially devastating to a civilian populous. Coriolanus's confidence feeds his rash self-righteousness (whether justified or not) and this is what makes him a monster. His rashness not his pride is what is monstrous.

The Beast with Many Heads

The people of Rome (plebs, tribunes, and senators) are also monstrous in that they let their fear feed their obsessive self-interests to the point where their social irresponsibility threatens to destroy the fabric of society. In the play the plebeians are presented in a monstrous form as *fragments* (1.1.221), as *discontented members* and *mutinous parts* (1.1.110). They are given shape through disease imagery as the *poor itch*, or *scabs* (1.1.165), and are cursed as *contagion*, carriers of *boils and plagues* (1.4.31) or referred to as *measles* (3.1.77).

The people are, just like Coriolanus, shown to be animals only this time the animals are of a domesticated type like *geese* (1.1171), *mules* (2.1.246), *camels* (2.1.250) and *a pack of curs* (1.1.167; 3.3.120). These are animals created to serve a master, unfortunately these particular animals are depicted as infectious, mutinous, and, like him, barely controllable (3.1.32; 34)

> *Are these your herd?*
> *You being their mouths, why rule you not their teeth?*

It is generally the tribunes that are assigned the role of " *the herdsmen of the beastly plebians*" (2.1.94-95) but they are a fractious bunch *"the mutable, rank-scented meinie"* (3.1.65) acting out in many directions as *"the beast with many heads"* (4.1.1) or the *"Hydra"* (3.1.92).

Monstrous, reeking, dissembled, and fragmented the people do not present a unified front but depict an assemblage of self-interests that are destructive to Rome. They are accused of being untrustworthy, easily frightened, and wavering (1.1.180-181)

> *Hang ye! Trust ye!*
> *With every minute you do change a mind.*

The argument against multiple self-interests is that it works against reason; it is unable to agree upon or stick to a plan and therefore sacrifices the good of the state to individual fears. Coriolanus fears that the people are individually lazy, fearful, and entitled refusing to give service in the wars for peace time benefits (3.1.121)

They ne'er did service for't.

He believes that *"their mutinies and revolts"* (3.1.125) during the war was not the *"kind of service"* that deserved *"corn gratis"* (3.1.123-124). He fears that the power they exert over government subverts the very government's ability to protect Rome (3.1.116)

I say they nourish'd disobedience, fed
The ruin of the state.

Coriolanus is not only concerned with 'fear guiding the populace' but also of the fear within the governing senate. Here Coriolanus speaks as if he were the people's voice (3.1.132-134)

We did request it,
We are the greater poll, and in true fear
They (the senate) *gave us our demands.*

Government by a fearful majority undermines careful reason (3.1.143-147)

...where gentry, title, wisdom,
Cannot conclude but by the yea and no
Of general ignorance, it must omit
Real necessities, and give way the while
To unstable slightness.

It is not, in fact, governing at all but merely administering to the ever changing whims of the people or *"the multidinous tongues"* (3.1.155).

This contradicts the advice given by Aristotle in his *Politics* (Book I, Part II)

> *"the city is before the house and every one of us...the whole is before the part: for if the whole perish there will remain neither foot nor hand".*

The people are not the only fearful faction but as seen above so are the senators. The senators fear the people and not without good cause, they fix grain prices, interest rates and change the laws to favour themselves (1.1.78-84). When Menenius tells his fable of the 'body politic' (the stomach supplying nutrients to the entire body) it is in fact a disconnect with the true state of affairs in the play. The body is not unified for we find Coriolanus is not part of the body at all nor are the plebeians equally supplied by the stomach. The fable is meant to entertain and distract from the reality of the situation, it is meant to pacify and delay the mob and avert a confrontation (1.1.161-162)

> *Rome and her rats are at the point of battle;*
> *The one side must have bale* (pain/sorrow).

The senate fears insurrection and is upbraided by Coriolanus several times for acquiescing to the people's demands (3.1.113;116)

> *Whoever gave that counsel, to give forth*
> *The corn o'th'storehouse gratis...*
> *I say they nourish'd disobedience, fed*
> *The ruin of the state.*

These signs of capitulation he feels led to his banishment (4.5.75-76;78-79)

> *The cruelty and envy of the people,*
> *Permitted by our dastard nobles, who*
> *...suffer'd me by the voice of slaves to be*
> *Whoop'd out of Rome.*

The controlling, manipulating tribunes also act out of fear, a fear of losing their positions and influence. Their self-interest feeds their fear that should Coriolanus become consul he will remove their positions (2.1.220-221)

> *Then our office may,*
> *During his power, go sleep.*

It is this fear that drives the tribunes to, in turn, inflame the people's fears of Coriolanus (2.1.243-246)

> *We must suggest the people in what hatred*
> *He still hath held them: that to's power he would*
> *Have made them mules, silenc'd their pleaders, and*
> *Dispropertied their freedoms.*

So in *Coriolanus* we find two monsters both existing at the extreme ends of Aristotle's dialectic. One finds expression through rashness, the other through fear. Corilanus's self-righteous over-confidence feeds his monstrous rashness and the people's (senators and tribunes included) fears feed their self-interests in such a way that the city cannot survive. Aristotle tells us in his *Politics* that moderation is required of all in order for a city to function.

> *"For except the governor be temperate and just, how will he govern well? Or if the subject be not, how shall he obey? Verily being intemperate and fearful, he will do nothing that is comely and meet (right/correct)."*

It is Aristotle's monsters of intemperance and fear that destroy Rome.

When Monsters Meet

Self-righteousness and self-interest grow to monstrous proportions in this drama. The intransigence of fundamentalism infects Coriolanus's virtues and although truth may be its bedrock his moral seriousness makes him both unappealing and insulting to others. Coriolanus chooses to serve Rome at the displeasure of its citizens. He hounds them in times of war and he hounds them in times of peace. He expects and demands the best of them at all times. He wants to see virtue and sacrifice from them and a concern for the good of others. He, adhering to Aristotelian ideals, wants to see them serve the city, the whole, before themselves (1.9.18-19)

> *He that has but effected his good will*
> *Hath overta'en mine act.*

He wants the citizens to be moved to action by upright intentions. He is willing to set the example (1.4.45)

> *Mark me, and do the like!*

and only asks that they try to do their individual best (1.9.15-16)

> *I have done*
> *As you have done, that's what I can.*

Coriolanus appears to be constantly at war. His default position is to oppose whatever is happening then step in and take charge. He does this numerous times; he takes over from Menenius, when Menenius has almost calmed the rioting plebeians, with his confrontational address to the crowd (1.1.164)

> *What's the matter, you dissentious rogues?*

His confrontational nature also stirs things up when he comes to assist Cominius, his fellow general (1.6.47-48)

> *Are you lords o'th'field?*
> *If not, why cease you till you are so?*

He is demanding of anyone that is less than they can be and particularly hard on anyone who asks him to be less than what he is. This striving for excellence in himself and others makes the people defensive and self-conscious of their own short comings. It in turn makes him appear arrogant and haughty as if he were the only one worthy of living in Rome (3.1.261-262)

> *Where is this viper*

That would depopulate the city and
Be everyman himself?

Volumnia and Menenius try to soften Coriolanus's means of expression after the people have rescinded their consent for his consulship (3.2). In essence they give him an acting lesson. This same acting lesson is employed by Volumnia on her son in the last act of the play so it is of special interest to both Shakespeare and the plot.

Coriolanus is a great-souled man dedicated to the truth so he is uncomfortable with adopting any form of gile (*Nicomachean Ethics*, IV.iii.28)

"*He must be open both in love and in hate, since concealment shows timidity; and care more for the truth than for what people will think; and speak and act openly*".

This is part of the reason he has trouble taking the advice of Volumnia and Menenius. Another reason lies in the belief held that 'action informed the mind'. E.R. Saunders in her paper *The Body of the Actor in 'Coriolanus'* points out some of the psychological difficulties that Coriolanus would have to overcome in order to adopt the advice given him. Many beliefs held about acting stem from thoughts expressed in Plato's *The Republic* (Book X, Theory of Art). In it he expresses the belief that poetry and drama infect the recipient and indulges their irrational (emotional) mind at the expense of their rational thought and by indulging it they exercise it and give it dominance over rationality (*The Republic*, Book X. 606d; 607a)

d. Poetry has the same effect on us when it represents sex and anger, and the other desires and feelings of pleasure and pain…It waters them…and makes them control us when we ought…to control them.

a. once you…admit the sweet lyric or epic muse, pleasure and pain become your rulers instead of law and the rational principles commonly accepted as best.

The same was true of acting. If you played the role of someone else (a villain or a troubled soul) it would change you by causing you to identify with an incorrect model of behavior and this action would leave an impression on your soul. Coriolanus fears that by compromising his values through any act of falsification, dissimulation or impersonation he may change his inner self; undermine his hard won identity that he carefully honed through a lifetime of honourable choices. Coriolanus, more than any other character in the play *is* what he has done. He has earned his name, his identity, through the action of conquering a city.

Volumnia wishes her son had some subtly in him, not been so outspoken, shown some restraint before the plebeians at least until they confirmed his appointment (3.2.21-23)

> *...if You had not show'd them how ye were dispos'd*
> *Ere they lack'd power to cross you.*

But now he must not just hide his opinions but he must apologize for voicing them. He must (3.2.36)

> *Repent what you have spoke.*

This is a near impossible task for Coriolanus to do, so Volumnia tries to prepare him for this by providing him with a script (3.2.52-57)

> *Because that now it lies you on to speak*
> *To th'people; not by your own instruction,*
> *Nor by th'matter which your heart prompts you,*
> *But with such words that are but roted in*
> *Your tongue, though but bastards and syllables*
> *Of no allowance to your bosom's truth.*

Knowing that the role will require not just words but also actions she gives him a choreography as well (3.2.72-76; 90-91)

> *Go to them, with this bonnet in thy hand...*
> *Thy knee bussing the stones – for in such business*
> *Action is eloquence, and the eyes of th'ignorant*

> *More learned than the ears – waving (bowing) thy head,*
> *Which often, thus, correcting thy stout heart,*
> *Now humble as the ripest mulberry*
> *That will not hold the handling; so say to them,*
> *Thou art their soldier...*
> *In asking, their good loves; but thou wilt frame*
> *Thyself, forsooth, hereafter theirs, so far*
> *As thou has power and person.*
> *Prithee now*
> *Go, and be rul'd.*

Coriolanus understands what he must do but the images he chooses in his reply tell us that it will not happen (3.2.99-101; 110-117)

> *Must I*
> *With my base tongue give to my noble heart*
> *A lie that it must bear? Well, I will do't:*
> *Well, I must do't.*
> *Away my disposition, and possess me*
> *Some harlot's spirit! My throat of war be turn'd,*
> *...into a pipe*
> *Small as an eunuch, or the virgin voice*
> *That babies lull asleep! The smiles of knaves*
> *Tent in my cheeks, and schoolboys' tears take up*
> *The glasses of my sight!*

The problem is that Coriolanus does not feel he has done any wrong, said anything that was untrue. He is the great-souled man *"incapable of living at the will of another"* (Nicomachean Ethics, IV.iii.29) and who cares *"more for the truth that for what people will think"* (Nicomachean Ethics, IV.iii.28). In the end we know Coriolanus is incapable to *"perform a part"* (3.2.109) for he fears it will compromise his very essence (3.2.120-123)

> *I will not do't,*
> *Lest I surcease to honour mine own truth,*
> *And by my body's action teach my mind*
> *A most inherent baseness.*

When Coriolanus meets with the people (self-righteousness clashes with self-interest) and things go badly just as planned by the tribunes who hoped to bait him by exploiting his rashness and insolence (2.1.254-255)

> *...that's as easy*
> *As to set dogs on sheep.*

The people, acting under the direction of the tribunes, recall their 'voice' or approval of Coriolanus as consul. This is a great insult to Coriolanus but he hopes to once again elicit their support by humbly performing the script given him by Volumnia.

To be offered the position of consul is a great honour which Coriolanus did not ask for (2.1.200-202)

> *Know, good mother,*
> *I had rather be their servant in my way*
> *Than sway* (rule) *with them in theirs.*

But it is an honour he is willing to receive (2.2.132)

> *The senate, Coriolanus, are well pleas'd*
> *To make thee consul.*

The people initially grant his elevation (2.3.154)

> *He has our voices, sir.*

But through coaxing of the Tribunes decide to withdraw their ascent (2.3.253)

> *...almost all*
> *Repent in their election.*

This act of eqivocation dishonours Coriolanus (3.1.57-59)

> *This palt'ring*

> *Becomes not Rome; nor has Coriolanus*
> *Deserv'd this so dishonour'd rub*

and again (3.3.58-61)

> *What is the matter*
> *That being pass'd for consul with full voice,*
> *I am so dishonour'd that the very hour*
> *You take it off again?*

It is an insult to a great-souled man and honour is the only thing that concerns the great-souled (*Nicomachean Ethics*, IV.iii.17)

"*Honour and dishonour then are the object with which the great-souled man is especially concerned. Great honours accorded by persons of worth will afford him pleasure in a moderate degree: he will feel he is receiving only what belongs to him...he will deign to accept their honours, because they have no greater tribute to offer him.*

He will despise dishonour, for no dishonour can justly attach to him".

It is this insult that turns Coriolanus against his own city. When they banish him (3.3.106) he in return banishes them (3.3.123). His response is fitting because Rome is the ideal, the city all citizens including Coriolanus serve. When they banish him, they banish the great-souled man, the equivalent of a prophet, the embodiment of virtue (*Nicomachean Ethics*, IV.iii.16)

"*Greatness of Soul seems therefore to be as it were a crowning ornament of the virtues*"

or (Nicomachean Ethics, IV.iii.17)

"*no honour can be adequate to the merits of perfect virtue*".

This act suggests that the people of Rome have banished virtue itself and are on the path away from the good.

When Coriolanus banishes them he is defending what Carson Holloway describes as the 'common good'. These people do not belong, have not earned, their place in Rome. As citizens they are not pulling their weight and so he is justified in banishing them.

When Coriolanus decides to attack Rome he sees himself as performing a cleansing action, removing those that call themselves Romans but are not willing to serve Her. It can be likened to God's judgment against a city (Sodom and Gomorrah), whose citizens have repudiated their commitment to virtue. Menenius concedes that Coriolanus's revenge is justified (5.4.31-35).

Following Coriolanus's banishment he no longer shows any flexibility (previously he dealt with the people's lack of service with insults and irony) he now adopts a fundamentalist approach to the problem – his way or no way. He acts without accommodation as if any moderation on his part would allow evil to coexist with virtue, an unacceptable compromise. He believes that he cannot trust the people and that they are ungrateful; they have neither earned their food nor their 'voice' through service to Rome. To receive benefits without reciprocating violates the fundamental requirement of living in a city, it shows ingratitude and it is from this 'seed of greed' that all crime grows. He feels justified like a "god to punish" the people of Rome.

Less Than Honourable Relations

"We blame a man as ambitious if he seeks honour more than is right" (*Nicomachean Ethics*, IV.iv.3).

In the play there are two characters that have a questionable relationship to honour and this manifests itself in a questionable relationship with Coriolanus. By questionable I mean not traditional. The first of these is the relationship between Volumnia and her son. Volumnia is not your typical mother, she is ambitious and she lives out that ambition through her son's actions. She is the mastermind behind his creation as a warrior (1.3.5-6; 14)

> *When yet he was*
> *but tender-bodied...*
> *To a cruel war I sent him.*

She delights in his accomplishments as if they were hers but she does not fear for his death, knowing that even in his death there is still his fame to benefit the family (1.3.20)

> *Then his good report should have been my son.*

She bathes in his reflected glory and it is the fame and glory and not a living son that matter to her. This is confirmed in one of her statements (1.3.21-25)

> *Hear me profess*
> *Sincerely: had I a dozen sons, each in my love alike,*
> *and none less dear than thine and my good Martius,*
> *I had rather had eleven die nobly for their country,*
> *than one voluptuously surfeit out of action.*

Volumnia is thankful when Coriolanus is injured (2.1.120)

> *Oh, he is wounded; I thank the gods for't.*

For she sees his wounds as a type of currency that will secure him a place in office (2.1 146-148)

> *...there will be*
> *large cicatrices* (scars) *to show the people when he shall*
> *stand for his place.*

Volumnia's concern is to turn Coriolanus's honourable actions into public acclaim, the form of which could be fame, good report, or even political office. She feels all her dreams are fulfilled when he is offered the position of consul (2.1.197-198)

> *I have liv'd*
> *To see inherited my very wishes.*

Unfortunately Coriolanus's sense of virtue interferes with her dreams. He has a hard time controlling his righteous anger and his rashness threatens his appointment. She councils him in the art of planning/scheming (3.2.29-31)

> *I have a heart as little apt as yours,*
> *But yet a brain that leads my use of anger*
> *To better vantage*

and deception (3.2.62-63)

> *I would dissemble with my nature where*
> *My fortunes and my friends at stake requir'd.*

She gives him an acting lesson that in turn foreshadows the role she will adopt at the end of the play. Her role as Rome's intercessor has as much to do with her own concerns as it does with the safety of Rome. When she appears before Coriolanus she manipulates him as she would have had him manipulate the citizens. I believe Coriolanus's response to her 'theatre piece' is sincere, as are all his actions in the play, but her pleas are tainted with an aspect of self-interest.

Her acting lesson to him and her plea can be compared. She instructs him to (3.2.73; 75-76)

> *Go to them, with this bonnet in thy hand*
> *Thy knee bussing the stones – for in such business*
> *Action is eloquence.*

She adopts this identical action when she comes before her son to plead for Rome (5.3.29-30)

> *My mother bows,*
> *As if Olympus to a molehill should*
> *in supplication nod.*

He responds to her act of submission by submitting himself (5.3.50)

> *Sink, my knee, i'th'earth* [Kneels].

She counters this move by submitting herself further, a parent kneeling to a child (5.3.53-55)

> *...with no softer cushion than the flint,*

> *I kneel before thee, and uproperly*
> *Show duty* [Kneels].

She enlists all the others (son, wife, Valeria) to kneel before him as well (5.3.77)

> *Even he, your wife, this lady and myself*
> *Are suiters to you.*

This reflects her advice to him given previously (3.2.80-81)

> *...or say to them,*
> *Thou art their soldier.*

She has orchestrated her performance before him just as she would have had him perform before the people. She has prepared costumes and choreography (5.3.94-96)

> *Should we be silent and not speak, our raiment*
> *And state of bodies would bewray what life*
> *We have led since thy exile.*

For she knows that in their suffering is their finest speech (3.2.76-79)

> *...the eyes of th' ignorant*
> *More learned than the ears – wavering thy head,*
> *Which often, thus, correcting thy stout heart,*
> *Now humble as the ripest mulberry.*

Coriolanus is moved by what he sees (bowing, kneeling, their physical state) more than by what he hears. He trusts actions more than words. Volumnia is careful that her request is fair. She does not ask him to compromise his honour (which is as precious to her as it is to him) but merely to broker a peace for *"The end of war's uncertain"* (5.3.141) for both sides so her *"suit is that you reconcile them"* (5.3.135-136). She also reminds him that there is no honour in this particular conquest for he will be remembered as one who destroyed his own mother-city (metropolis) Rome (5.3.145-148)

> *The man was noble,*

> *But with his last attempt he wip'd it out,*
> *Destroy'd his country, and his name remains*
> *To th'insuing age abhorr'd.*

This last threat probably means nothing to Coriolanus but it means everything to Volumnia who has been and will be living off his reflected honour for years to come, if it remains intact. It is she that fears losing his good name (he will merely forge a new one for himself *"o'th'fire of burning Rome"* (5.1.14)).

She has however moved him – reintroduced him to his wife and son – reminded him that he is a part of a greater whole. In spite of his self-sufficiency he is but a fragment of his family. She gave him life, made him her legacy; all he is ultimately is because of her. There are things he has taken from his mother and things he will give to his son. The dance of give and take is the source of all honour and so he becomes aware of the debt he owes to posterity and the dishonour that would be associated with familial destruction.

Volumnia has accomplished her task through acting, a form of deceit, but more importantly she has made Coriolanus act. She made him kneel, as a son should do before a mother, she made him act the father by eliciting advice from him for his son (5.3.70; 71-74)

> *The god of soldiers,*
> *...inform*
> *Thy thoughts with nobleness, that thou mayst prove*
> *To shame unvulnerable, and stick i'th'wars*
> *Like a great sea-mark standing every flaw*
> *And saving those that eye thee!*

By acting like a son, a father, he has become one. He is no longer just the dragon. The greatest fear Coriolanus harboured about acting has proven true (3.2.122)

> *...my body's action teach my mind.*

This reverse transformation marks a return to his honourable self. The request his mother makes (though self-motivated) is the honourable course of action not just for Romans but for the Volscians too. As such Coriolanus's last act is one that provides justice to all (*Nicomachean Ethics*, V.i.15).

"*Justice then in this sense is perfect Virtue...it is displayed towards others. This is why Justice is often thought to be the chief of the virtues...and we have the proverb*

In Justice is all Virtue found in sum."

Coriolanus is aware that some Volscians are not interested in peace and will see the act as a betrayal by him. He knows his life is in peril (5.3.186-189)

You have won a happy victory to Rome;
But for your son, believe it, O, believe it,
Most dangerously you have with him prevail'd
If not most mortal to him. But let it come.

He does his best to mitigate against any backlash by having Aufidius frame the treaty (5.3.197)

What peace you'll make, advise me.

Whether his mother recognizes the danger she has placed her son in or whether she pays any attention to his statement is in the director's hands but the result is that she comes away from the meeting inheiriting all the Honour that was due her son. It is she who returns to Rome as its saviour (5.5.1)

Behold our patroness, the life of Rome!

Volumnia receives what her son could not, the praise of an entire city (5.4.53-55).

This Volumnia
Is worth of consuls, senators, patricians,
A city full.

Whether her son lives or dies is irrelevant to her; she has preserved *"his good report"* and she has preserved Rome. She has also achieved her personal dream of Fame and Glory.

Volumnia's unnatural relationship with Honour (Coriolanus) is best revealed when we first meet her. It is through the incestuous imagery she employs when speaking of Maritus that we recognize something is askew (1.3.2-4)

> *If my son were my husband*
> *I should freelier rejoice in that absence wherein he*
> *Won honour, than in the embrassments of his bed.*

It reveals an obsession with honour over human contact. From Aristotle we know honour only comes from virtue and a concern for others. She has mistaken fame and glory for honour (which is bound to service) and is willing to sacrifice her children in order to obtain it. She wishes to receive the public's response to honour which comes in the form of adulation rather than perform the service to the public which is the source of the honour.

Aufidius, like Volumnia, does not care so much for honour as those things that follow from it. Coriolanus is his sworn enemy and he wishes him dead by hook or by crook and says just that (1.10.7-10; 12-16)

> *Five times, Martius,*
> *I have fought thee; so often hast thou beat me;*
> *And would do so, I think, should we encounter*
> *As often as we eat.*
> *Mine emulation* (desire to equal him)
> *Hath not that honour in't it had: for where*
> *I thought to crush him in an equal force,*
> *True sword to sword, I'll potch* (poke) *at him some way,*
> *Or wrath or craft may get him.*

Aufidius has given up the idea of honourable battle with Coriolanus; he admits his *"valour's poison'd"* (1.10.17). He intends to kill Coriolanus by any means possible even if it means violating the canon of hospitality (1.10.25), i.e., killing a guest. To act dishonestly is in direct violation of what it means to be honourable (*Nicomachean Ethics*, IV.iii.15)

"For instance, one cannot imagine the great-souled man...acting dishonestly".

Aufidius is in fact envious of a man who has literally nothing but honour (no home, no family, no fortune). When Coriolanus returns after declaring peace with Rome it is he who is greeted by cheering crowds whereas no such welcome is given to Aufidius (5.6.50-52)

Your native home you enter'd like a post,
And had no welcome home; but he returns
Splitting the air with noise.

Aufidius uses Coriolanus to conquer Rome and then plans to displace him as *"One fire drives out one fire; one nail, one nail"* (4.7.54). He will then take over his position. This action is not unlike Volumnia's own plan of displacing Coriolanus's honour onto herself. Aufidius plans Coriolanus's death to occur in tandem with his own advancement (5.6.48-49)

Therefore shall he die,
And I'll renew me in his fall.

Both Volumnia and Aufidius see honour as a commodity that can be monetized or passed on. For them honour can be traded for position and power; it can be upgraded from its humble origin in virtue and service. Coriolanus stands in the right relationship with honour for he *"rewards his deeds with doing them"* (2.2.127-128).

Volumnia and Aufidius reflect an excessive desire for honour. In Volumnia it manifests itself as a type of vanity (*Nicomachean Ethics*, II.vii.7)

"In respect of honour and dishonour, the observance of the mean is Greatness of Soul, the excess a sort of Vanity".

In Aufidius this excessive drive for great honours is called ambition (*Nicomachean Ethics*, II.vii.8)

"he who exceeds in these aspirations is called ambitious".

Aufidius's excessive desire to surmount Coriolanus gives rise to homoerotic dreams of domination (4.5.123-127)

I have nightly since
Dreamt of encounters 'twixt thyself and me –
We have been down together in my sleep,
Unbuckling helms, fisting each other's throat –
And wak'd half dead with nothing.

Both Volumnia and Aufidius admire Coriolanus but also view him as politically inept. They will both use him and discard him; for what they truly value is adulation, money and power. They are as badly infected with the gangrene of self-interest as any others in the play.

The Great Silence

One relationship that is honourable is that between Coriolanus and his wife, Virgilia. I believe Shakespeare's intention for Virgilia (Vir. in the script) is to have her play the role of Virtue; for Virtue is married to Honour (*The French Academie*, (1598), Primaudaye, p.246-247)

"For this cause the ancient Romans built two Temples joined together, the one being dedicated to Virtue, and the other to Honour: but yet in such sort, that no man could enter into that of Honour, except first he passed through the other of Virtue".

There is an expression that 'Virtue is silent' in that it does not blow its own horn or draw attention to itself. Virtue is a verb, it is an action, it is performed for the good of others. Virgilia is an essentially silent character who is often described as being dominated by her mother-in-law. Although Volumnia is a force to be reckoned with I would argue that she does not control Virgilia, for instance, Virgilia chooses to act in consort with her husband by staying indoors while he is on the battlefield (1.3.74-75)

> *I'll not over the*
> *Threshold till my lord returns from the wars.*

It is a symbolic act of unity performed to support her husband, a private sacrifice to show she shares in his suffering. Volumnia cannot convince her to join them (Volumnia and Valeria) on a day out so instead dismisses her with an insult (1.3.103-104)

> *Let her alone, lady; as she is now, she will but*
> *Disease our better mirth.*

Interestingly virtue is seen as a disease of mirth, just as Coriolanus (virtue embodied) is seen as a disease (gangrene) and is banished by the lazy citizens of Rome.

Virgilia is one of the few characters that behaves as one would expect; instead of rejoicing in Coriolanus's wounds as Volumnia does, she cries and worries for his safety. She wishes the best for her husband (2.1.173-176)

> Vol.: *But oh, thy wife –*
> Cor.: *My gracious silence, hail!*
> *Wouldst thou have laugh'd had I come coffin'd home,*
> *That weep'st to see me triumph?*

Coriolanus's nickname for his wife is 'silence'. This is what makes her such an interesting contrast to the plebeians who do little but talk, complain and 'voice' throughout the play (*The French Academie*, (1598), P.de la Primandaye, p. 133)

"Further we must know that silence in due time and place, is profound wisdom, a sober and modest thing, and full of deep secrets."

Virgilia is not meek but speaks her mind to both the Tribunes and to Volumnia. She like the great-souled man is frugle with words (*Nicomachean Ethics*, IV.iii.31)

"He is no gossip, for he will not talk either about himself or about another, as he neither wants to receive compliments nor to hear other people run down".

Virgilia and Coriolanus at times share this trait of silence. Her silence reflects wisdom whereas his silence reflects determination. We see this when he is depicted as a force of nature, like the silent eye of a hurricane, where all around him is noise and chaos (2.1.157-158)

before him he
carries noise, and behind him he leaves tears.

Two Gods

Aristotle said that only gods or beasts are not fit for life in the city. With Martius Coriolanus we are faced with a self-sufficient individual who is as close to a god as anyone in the play, but not just any god, he is likened to Mars himself (4.5.119)

Why, thou Mars!

And again (4.5.196-197)

As if he
were son and heir to Mars.

Mars, Ares, the god of war, is certainly a god, certainly deserving of honour but not the kind of god that could ever be accommodated in a city; destroying harmony, creating strife and chaos, acting as a destabilizing force in general.

That Mars was a model for Martius is of little doubt (*New Larousse Encyclopedia of Mythology*, p. 124, 202, 204). They share a similar backstory in that neither had a father. Mars was the son of Juno/Hera (Protectress of the Roman people) who gave birth to him autonomously, without the assistance of Jupiter, but rather by means of a flower. Mars was the most Roman of the gods (he was father to Romulus and Remus, the founders of Rome) who instilled in the people the virtues of honour and courage. But despite these attributes Zeus/Jupiter never spoke highly of Mars, in the Illiad he says of Ares

"Of all the gods who live on Olympus thou art the most odious to me; for thou enjoyest nothing but strife, war and battles. Thou hast the obstinate and unmanageable disposition of thy mother Hera, whom I can scarcely control with my words".

This inability of words to control Mars brings us back to Shakespeare's play where words are incapable of controlling Martius Coriolanus. The use of words in the play also reveals the secret presence of another god, Hermes/Mercury. Hermes was the god of eloquence and also the god of the marketplace (*New Larousse Encyclopedia of Mythology*, p. 123, 207); a divinity to overlook profit, both lawful and unlawful. He was both a god of commerce and a god to thieves. His eloquence was used to facilitate business by overcoming a buyer's hesitation with subtle and persuasive words. His eloquence and deception was also associated with politics and political scheming.

So in this play we have two gods Mars and Mercury just as we have two monsters, self-righteousness and self-interest. Neither monster and neither god is capable of living in a city.

Words and Actions

In Shakespeare's play words are used in an attempt to control action. In the drama people fall into two distinct types: those that use words, like the senators (1.1.88-89)

I shall tell you
A pretty tale

and the citizens (1.1.1)

...hear me speak

and those that use action, like Martius Coriolanus (1.4.45)

Mark me, and do the like!

However neither words nor actions can claim the moral high ground since words can be used to deceive and manipulate others just as actions can. The two are interdependent (*The Life of Caius Martius Coriolanus*, Plutarch)

"For the soule, nor god himselfe can distinctly speake without a bodie".

Both words and actions require a body for expression; speech and action are physical manifestations of an inner intent. Speech, in the play, is used to communicate but it is also used to delay or coordinate action. The play begins with this sentiment (1.1.1)

Before we proceed any further, hear me speak.

Deliberation before action is a sign of prudence but once consultation is over then appropriate actions should proceed (1.1.11)

No more talking on't; let it be done.

The mob resolved to do its task is then confronted by Menenius who turns their complaint of 'empty bellies' to rhetorical purposes by telling them *"a pretty tale"* wherein their arguments are turned to a different conclusion (*The Controversial Eloquence of Shakespeare's Coriolanus*, West and Silberstein). Menenius takes their complaint that food is not being distributed to them by the patricians and inverts it into a parable of social harmony wherein the patricians now figure as a generous belly that supplies all the body politic's members with nourishment leaving themselves only the bran.

It is a ludicrous tale leisurely told whose purpose is to slow the crowd down and prevent it from linking up with other like-minded groups. Menenius wishes to avoid any escalating violence and does so by entertaining and distracting the crowd; he hopes his tale and the pacing of it will lull the crowd from their initial purpose (1.1.200)

...these are almost thoroughly persuaded.

The entrance of Martius Coriolanus re-ignites the crowd. He employs a hard, brittle, cutting and confrontational style of rhetoric. It is the verbal equivalent of his no-nonsense military actions. Coriolanus who is Spartan in his affectations is deeply suspicious of language which he sees as generally deceptive. For him actions take precedence over words; it is actions he trusts.

Words, Actions, Deception, and Violence

The divide between words and actions is an artificial one, both are acts of the body, both can be used to communicate, both can be used to deceive, both can be used for violent purposes, and both can serve the greater good. All these actions (for speech is an action) are controlled by the mind (rational or irrational) and subject to moral judgment (*Nicomachean Ethics*, III.i.1)

"Virtue however is concerned with emotions and actions, and it is only voluntary actions for which praise and blame are given".

Both words and actions are equally corrupt and corruptible. When the mob is convinced to riot it is Menenius who calms them and Coriolanus who dismisses them (1.1.221)

Go get you home, you fragments!

The mob, here and throughout the play, is an eminently mobile lot, for a mob is by definition mobile, unstable, and changeable. They represent a force that can be manipulated by lies or threats to support a particular action. Their commitment to that action is shallow and never amounts to anymore than their consent or their voice. They do however because of their number represent a sizable threat if ever they chose to commit to a purpose. It is this potential for unity, for wholeness that gives them power.

The patricians, senators and tribunes all use deception to control and direct the mob. Menenius tells them tales of unity and interdependence. The tribunes manipulate the people through a combination of suggestion (2.3.198-201) and deception (2.3.224-227). Aufidius too elicits mob support by lying to them of Coriolanus's duplicity (5.6.85). Coriolanus, being more open, does not enlist deception but rather uses the verbal equivalent of a fist when he threatens the mob with violence (1.1.196-199)

> *Would the nobility lay aside their ruth,* (pity)
> *And let me use my sword, I'd make a quarry*
> *With thousands of these quarter'd slaves, as high*
> *As I could pick my lance.*

All are trying to control the mob in some way, some for selfish reasons (to protect their positions) and some for more noble reasons (to support the state) but public opinion is being courted continuously and from all sides.

This manipulation by deception and violence is not just being done through words but it is also done through actions. The senators press people into service (1.1.223-225) by shipping them off to foreign wars, for example against the Volsces. This practice is used to ship off 'trouble-makers' and ease sedition at home. The physical removal of persons becomes the means to manipulate the popular voice.

Deception is also practiced through actions or more precisely through performance. Volumnia gives Coriolanus a lesson on how to appear and act humble (3.2). The lesson does not take but the message is clear; all public behaviour is to some extent acting since physical demeanor can carry part of the message. Both eyes and ears (more fragmented body parts) are equally prone to manipulation.

At the heart of all the manipulations in the play are people's self-interests. By appealing to or threatening the self-interests of the party to be manipulated (verbally or by actions) one can generally achieve one's goal. This, of course, is what passes for politics in Rome. Politics is, as Zui Jagendorf insists, a dance between division and unity; fragmentation and wholeness. In the beginning humans had to decide whether to live on their own, following their own self-interests, or live in communities where shared interests may clash with individual concerns. Communities have the same needs as the individual but they are writ-large. Food, shelter, security are the issues in both worlds but sometimes the 'body-politic' requires sacrifices from the individual to protect the whole.

A city is made up of a great number of people doing different jobs, belonging to different classes. They make up an uneasy association of disparate needs, so at any given time the sacrifices made by one group may be disproportionate to the benefits they receive. This causes fragmentation of the whole and if these divisions are not corrected it can lead to the complete breakdown of the whole.

Politics uses all the means of manipulation available to them in order to keep people working together; preventing the fragmentation that is counterproductive to the whole. Because city-states are closed systems it means that the affluence of one class is built on the suffering of another (1.1.15; 19-21)

What authority surfeits on would relieve us.
...our misery, is

> *as an inventory to particularize their abundance;*
> *our sufferance is a gain to them.*

This is why the metaphor for the body is such a strong one and why Shakespeare chose to explore this idea in much of his imagery. The Rome we see is much more fragmented than it is whole or healthy. It is rife with internal strife and class hatred. The play is full of body parts, limbs, legs, arms, tongues, scabs, wounds, mouths, teeth, voices, bellies, and toes. It is equally full of bodily actions like eating, vomiting, starving, beating, scratching, wrestling, piercing, etc. Menenius's tale depicting the orthodoxy of unity does not apply to Rome which at this point is fragmented into parts and not functioning as a healthy whole. The parts are too self-interested to be fair to one another (every man for himself) and therefore are incapable of trusting one another. Without trust there can be no bonds and without bonds there can be no community. Those managing the society appear to be more willing to sacrifice its parts than they are to look for a cure to its troubles (3.1.292-294)

> Sic.: *He's a disease that must be cut away.*
> Men.: *Oh, he's a limb that has but a disease:*
> *Mortal, to cut it off; to cure it easy.*

The bonds that need to be formed in order to create a community are being displaced by the competition of the marketplace. Self-interest is displacing shared concerns. The disintegration of the body into fragments is a repetitive and horrific image that is related to the rise of self-interests as seen in a fixed marketplace (monopolies, price fixing, loan sharking) (1.1.79-85). The people feel their lives are threatened both outside and inside by a type of internal cannibalism

> *If the wars eat us not up, they will.*

The senators appear to be the instigators of this trickle-down selfishness. They pass the laws that can press the citizens into military service and they control the access to both money and food. There appears to be a policy by the rulers to keep the citizens hungry and therefore compliant, with any disobedience being dealt with by military force.

The result of these policies is a selfish citizenry, trying to protect the little they have, and expending as little effort as possible to help one another. The city is breaking apart in an 'everyman for himself' fashion. Cooperative harmony has devolved into beastly selfishness.

The Marketplace

A city is held together by the politics of continual negotiation; like the marketplace these negotiations require a 'tit for tat' act of exchange. No one part can be seen as unfairly benefiting at the expense of another. The process must be transparent, public, and seen by the public as fair. The exchanges create bonds between the parties involved; if the exchanges meet each of the participant's needs (and political exchanges are not always financial) then they come to know what each side values. To be known is to be seen and considered and at its most basic level represents a form of respect.

Coriolanus does not wish to play any part in the market economy. He resents what he does for the good of the state to be considered a labour done for payment. When offered one-tenth of all the booty recovered in the war he declines (1.9.36-38)

>*I thank you general;*
>*But cannot make my heart consent to take*
>*A bribe to pay my sword: I do refuse it.*

For him service is its own reward (2.2.127-128)

>(He) *rewards*
>*His deeds with doing them.*

Politics is a form of exchange, even Aristotle makes this point (*Nicomachean Ethics*, V.i.16)

'Office will show a man'; for in office one is brought into relation with others and becomes a member of a community.

Coriolanus, because of his unchangeable nature, cannot participate in the 'tit for tat' exchanges required of him (*Nicomachean Ethics*, IV.iii.26)

It is also characteristic of the great-souled man never to ask help from others, or only with reluctance, but to render aid willingly.

This isolates him from other members of the community. They do not know him nor does he know them. This lack of mutual understanding leads to a communication breakdown in the marketplace scene where he is required to show them his wounds and to ask for their voice of assent. Coriolanus fears that the display of his wounds would, by providing a 'show' for them turn his scars (marks of actual service and sacrifice) into marketing symbols to buy votes (2.2.147-150)

> *To brag unto them, thus I did, and thus,*
> *Show them th'unaching scars which I should hide,*
> *As if I had receiv'd them for the hire*
> *Of their breath only.*

The people respect Coriolanus, they understand that his appointment is a gesture that pales in comparison to the service he has given and the financial rewards he has turned down. They do not wish to show ingratitude and feel morally they have no choice (2.3.1-2; 4-5; 39-40)

> Cit. 1: *Once, if he do require our voices, we ought not*
> *To deny him.*
> Cit. 3: *We have power in ourselves to do it, but it is*
> *A power that we have no power to do.*
> *...if he would incline to the people, there was*
> *never a worthier man.*

Coriolanus has a very jaundiced view of the people. He like Menenius and Volumnia (2.1.146-148), thinks his wounds are seen by the people as a currency to be exchanged for their votes. He finds it degrading to ask the people for help: it puts him in an inferior position. The disgust he feels is conjured up by one of the citizens (2.3.5-8)

> *For, if he*
> *show us his wounds and tell us his deeds, we are to*
> *put our tongues into those wounds and speak for*
> *them.*

This bond-building requires a sense of intimacy he is uncomfortable with especially when he regards them as no better than slaves *"woolen vassels, things created To buy and sell with groats"* (3.2.9-10). He thinks the consulship comes with a price and that price is to come begging (2.3.70-71)

> *No, sir, 'twas never my desire yet to trouble the*
> *poor with begging.*

But his impression is mistaken, the people just want to see him, see that he is one of them, see if he will show them respect (2.3.75)

> *The price is, to ask it kindly.*

The people view their voice just as Coriolanus views his service, as something that is not for sale, and they are insulted by his insinuation that it is (2.3.72-73)

> *You must think, if we give you anything, we*
> *hope to gain by you.*

The two sides have different expectations of one another and fail to communicate. Coriolanus thinks they need to see his wounds because they do not trust him. The plebeians become 'doubting Thomases' in Coriolanus's mind that do not believe his word. The people, on the other hand, think Coriolanus sees them as beggars who would sell their vote to the highest bidder. Because of this lack of insight both sides are insulted and instead of bonds being built divisions are created.

It is these divisions, if exploited, which cause societal breakdown. This particular division is exploited by the tribunes to banish Coriolanus (the man who threatens their jobs) from Rome. Aufidius later will exploit a division he believes exists within Coriolanus in order to plot his death (5.3.199-202)

> *I am glad thou hast set thy mercy and thy*
> *Honour*
> *At difference in thee. Out of that I'll work*
> *Myself a former fortune.*

Divisions destroy unity while bonds preserve it. When Coriolanus has grown *"from man to dragon"* (5.4.13) he breaks all bonds with Rome, friends and family (5.1.12-13)

> *(He) forbad all names:*
> *he was a kind of nothing, titleless*

(5.1.80)

> *Wife, mother, child, I know not.*

He strips himself of all his humanity (5.3.24-25)

> *But out, affection!*
> *All bond and privilege of nature break!*

And vows to behave as an autonomous creature removed from his fellow humans (5.3.35-37)

> *but stand*
> *As if a man were author of himself*
> *And knew no other kin.*

With all bonds broken he becomes a thing (5.4.18-22)

> *When he walks, he*
> *moves like an engine and the ground shrinks before*
> *his treading. He is able to pierce a corslet with his*

> *eye, talks like a knell, and his hum is a battery. He*
> *sits in his state as a thing made for Alexander.*

His disengagement with society has been gradual but it has been in step with Rome's own dissolution. He becomes more autonomous just as the citizens of Rome become more self-interested. Coriolanus literally becomes author of himself with the taking of Corioli (1.9.61-62;63)

> *And from this time,*
> *For what he did before Corioles, call him,*
> *Martius Caius Coriolanus!*

Coriolanus is never deeply integrated into his society but he has ties to his fellow soldiers, some senators, and his family but these few ties are severed when he is banished. The banishment also marks a supreme act of selfishness on the part of Rome. Symbolically they have cast out the representative of 'selfless acts of service to the state'. By banishing him they have condemned themselves to live in a fragmented dog-eat-dog collective that has merely the appearance of a city.

Among the Volcians Coriolanus completes his evolution and disengages completely with humanity (5.4.12-14)

> *This Martius is*
> *grown from man to dragon: he has wings: he's more*
> *than a creeping thing.*

He becomes the embodiment of autonomy and he destroys Rome from the outside just as the self-interested parties destroy Rome from the inside. It is only by re-establishing some familial bonds that Volumnia manages to turn the 'thing' back into human form. By reminding him of his connections and obligations to his wife and son he becomes part of a family unit. Becoming part of a whole requires sacrifice by all its members and he knows his choice may be mortal to himself (5.3.187-189). His sacrifice is just enough to save Rome from its immediate external threat but for Rome to survive every member must learn the lesson of sacrifice and build bonds of trust by ending their mutual exploitation of one another and the system.

The play ends on a very bitter note; Coriolanus the symbol of service to the state is killed under the chant of *"Tear him to pieces"* (5.6.120). He is reduced to fragments, and then eulogized by the man who manipulated and lied about him. It marks the triumph of the 'fragments', the self-interested, over the whole and leaves us with a feeling of despair.

Conclusion

The tragedy that besets *Coriolanus* is one that is characterized by the processes of both fragmentation of the whole and the act of existing autonomously. Both, in essence, are examples of the same phenomenon. When a society fragments it is because those individuals that make up that society no longer see themselves as part of the greater whole. They have become so self-interested that all they care about is themselves; they have in fact become autonomous without first becoming self-sufficient. This lack of independence means they now prey on others within their own society. They are the internal parasites that cannibalize their society from within. They take from their society but do not give back to their society. Internally they are breaking the bonds that hold society together. Their exploitative actions show ingratitude, they no longer respect the rules of give and take, and they no longer believe that the benefits they receive by living in a collective are worthy of any kind of reciprocation. All the people of Rome –senators, tribunes and common citizens - manifest this self-interest. They all take but resent having to give back.

Coriolanus is also an example of this same trait, possessing an autonomous nature, but he differs from the rest because he is both self-made and self-sufficient. He does not require anything from anybody and so he is not predatory or selfish. He in fact serves the whole with a zealousness that permits little criticism. He represents the awful virtues of hard work, dedication, and sacrifice. He demands this of himself and of others. He is a hard-ass that expects others to pull their weight, to serve society. He is upset when people ask for what they have not earned or when they act against the interests of the state. His self-righteousness permits no dialogue and he stands in harsh judgment of those around him. His critical and extreme nature can best be accommodated on a battlefield but it proves to be a poor fit as part of a collective society. He, like an Old Testament prophet, is supportive of the ideals of a society but has little tolerance for those that fall short of perfection.

Because of his self-sufficiency Coriolanus is a character that cannot be controlled with words and because of his indignation and open nature he cannot control his own words. His fundamentalist self-righteousness drives his autonomy and precludes any involvement in the economy of give and take that is so necessary in society. He cannot easily build bonds with others.

Society, as depicted in the play, is fragmented with senators and tribunes preying on the people and the people, if not for the rule of law, *"would feed on one another"* (1.1.187). The infection that is cannibalizing the city is one of self-interest. It has created a fragmented collective of self-entitled individuals, who take what they can and that are no longer capable of making any of the sacrifices necessary to maintain a society. The bonds of reciprocity are broken and the Roman people are left to suffer from the diseases of want (the hungry plebeians) and those of excess (the senators).

The play is apocalyptic in nature. It ends on a hopeless note but its structure reveals a surprisingly Christian message within. Zui Jagendorf points out that Menenius's fable of the body politic has a Christian equivalent found in *I Corinthians 12* (12-27). Paul's parable differs from

Menenius's in that it starts with the concept that the body parts are equal but different. The stress is on the inclusion and celebration of difference rather than on hierarchy.

12 For as the body is one, and hath many members, and all the members of that one body, being many, are one body: so also is Christ.

13 For by one Spirit are we all baptized into one body...

16 And if the ear shall say, Because I am not the eye, I am not of the body; is it therefore not of the body?

17 If the whole body were an eye, where were the hearing?

20 But now are they many members, yet but one body.

25 ...there should be no schism in the body; but that the members should have the same care one for another.

26 And whether one member suffer, all the members suffer with it; or one member be honoured, all the members rejoice with it.

27 Now ye are the body of Christ, and members in particular.

The Christian ethic, if adhered to, could keep a community united whereas Menenius's fable does not find resonance with the citizens' concerns nor does it reflect their reality; the belly of Rome's senate is not sharing. Rome is not working as a collective. Shakespeare's nod to a biblical analog may suggest a possible alternative to the particular dystopia unfolding in his play.

The choice of the body as the central image and the constant repetition of body parts and functions throughout the work informs us that these are carefully crafted images intentionally chosen to fit within a particular program.

Rome is presented as a state that does not nourish its citizens and Volumnia is presented as a mother that did not nourish any humanity in Martius. The two, the multi-headed mob and Coriolanus, are two monsters created by two different mothers. The first, the mob, is capable of destroying Rome from within and the second is capable of destroying it from without. Both are autonomous beasts that are robbed of their ability to connect or bond with others. The citizens lose this ability through the increased selfishness, self-interest, and self-protection that is required of them to survive in a community where they are exploited like farm animals by the senate and their own representatives - the tribunes.

Coriolanus loses this ability (if he ever had it) to relate to or bond with others through his upbringing in the wars. Celebrated and rewarded for his most anti-social tendencies it is not surprising he views others, who do not share his views of service to the state, as disposable enemies.

The citizens and Martius Coriolanus are the extreme manifestations of a single dialectic; the dynamic which exists between fear and confidence. The plebs fear for their very survival and their fear drives their selfishness and their instinct to protect themselves over their fellows. This fear destabilizes the city because it tears down the bonds that hold communities together. An 'everyman for himself' philosophy overrides the feelings of mutual support and sacrifice necessary to keep a city functioning.

Coriolanus represents the other end of the dynamic - excess confidence. He fears nothing, but like the plebs, he isolates himself only in his case it is through self-sufficiency and self-righteousness. He is incapable of interacting in any kind of 'give and take' manner with others for he needs nothing from anyone. Because of this he exists outside of politics and therefore, at least metaphorically, outside the city. As long as he serves the state and minds his own business he is seen as an asset but when he is given the chance to wield political power as a consul he is then seen as a threat by the citizenry. The citizens are unable to relate to him as a person or to his zealous belief in service and so, acting out of their fears and self-interests, they banish him as a danger to the people. In the process they create Rome's greatest external threat.

Rome survives the play but only because Coriolanus reconnects with his family and the concept of reciprocity; for the gifts he has received, for the life he has been given *"Thou are my warrior: I holp to frame thee"* (5.3.63) he feels a duty to be grateful and to give back. He owes his mother, wife and son a service and to his family, writ-large Rome, he also owes a debt. Coriolanus, the thing, becomes once more Coriolanus, the man. Once more he shows the Roman people through his actions what they must do *"Mark me, and do the like!"* (1.4.45). Bonds must be reformed, the fairness of reciprocity reestablished, and sacrifices must be made.

Bibliography

1) *Coriolanus*, W. Shakespeare, The Arden Shakespeare, edited by Philip Brockbank, Routledge, 1990.
2) *Nicomachean Ethics*, Aristotle, The Loeb Classical Library, edited by Jeffrey Henderson, English translation by H. Rackham, Harvard University Press, 1934.
3) *Shakespeare's 'Coriolanus' and Aristotle's Great-Souled Man*, Carson Holloway, *The Review of Politics*, Vol. 69, No.3, Special Issue on Politics and Literature (Summer, 2007), p. 353-374.
4) *Coriolanus, Aristotle and Bacon*, F.N. Lees, *The Review of English Studies*, New Series, Vol. 1, No. 2 (April, 1950), p. 114-125.
5) *The Coming Robot Revolution; Expectation and Fear About Emerging Intelligent, Humanlike Machines*, Yoseph Bar-Cohen and David Hanson, Springer, 2009.
6) *The Body of the Actor in 'Coriolanus'*, Eve Rachele Sanders, *Shakespeare Quarterly*, Vol.57, No. 4 (Winter 2006), p. 287-412.
7) *Shakespeare's Imagery and What it Tells Us*, Caroline Spurgeon, Cambridge University Press, 1935.
8) *Animal Imagery in 'Coriolanus'*, J.C. Maxwell, *The Modern Language Review*, Vol. 42, No. 4 (October, 1947), p.417-421.
9) *Suffocating Mothers; Fantasies of Maternal Origin in Shakespeare's Plays, Hamlet to the Tempest*, Janet Adelman, Chapter 6, Escaping the Matrix: The Construction of Masculinity in *Macbeth* and *Coriolanus*, p. 130-165, Routledge, 1992.
10) *The Controversial Eloquence of Shakespeare's Coriolanus – an Anti-Ciceronian Orator?*, Michael West and Myron Silberstein, *Modern Philology*, Vol. 102, No. 3 (February 2005), p. 307-331.
11) *Coriolanus: Body Politic and Private Parts*, Zui Jagendorf, *Shakespeare Quarterly*, Vol. 41, No. 4 (Winter, 1990), p. 455-469.

12) *The Failure of Words*, Carol M. Sicherman, ELM, Vol. 39, No. 2 (June, 1972), p. 189-207.
13) *New Larousse Encyclopedia of Mythology*, transl. Richard Aldington and Delano Ames, edited by Felix Guirand, The Hamlyn Publishing Group Ltd., 16th edition, 1982.
14) *The French Academie* (1586), Peter de la Primaudaye, facsimilie of copy in the British Museum shelfmark: 84.06.ee.25, translation by T. B[owes], Georg Olms Verlag, 1972.
15) *The Imperial Theme, Further Interpretations of Shakespeare's Tragedies including the Roman Plays*, Chapter 6 The Royal Occupation: An Essay on Coriolanus, G. Wilson Knight, Methuen and Company Ltd., 1954, p. 154-199.
16) *The Republic*, Plato, translated by Desmond Lee, Penguin Classics, 2007.

www.ingramcontent.com/pod-product-compliance
Lightning Source LLC
Chambersburg PA
CBHW061429040426
42450CB00007B/966